This is the complete, unabridged text of the briefs filed by the U. S. House of Representatives and the lawyers for the defense of Donald J. Trump, former President of the United States of America, in the second impeachment trial of same.

The first document is the brief filed by the U. S. House Managers February 2, 2021; it is followed by the brief filed by the defense on February 8, 2021, and the reply thereto filed the same day by the U. S. House Managers.

These documents are hereby published by Integral Text Publishing, edited and arranged by Sky Pelletier Waterpeace, as a service to those who may find them valuable.

IN THE SENATE OF THE UNITED STATES
Sitting as a Court of Impeachment

In re

IMPEACHMENT OF
PRESIDENT DONALD J. TRUMP

TRIAL MEMORANDUM OF THE UNITED STATES HOUSE OF REPRESENTATIVES IN THE IMPEACHMENT TRIAL OF PRESIDENT DONALD J. TRUMP

United States House of Representatives

Jamie Raskin
Diana DeGette
David Cicilline
Joaquin Castro
Eric Swalwell
Ted Lieu
Stacey Plaskett
Madeleine Dean
Joe Neguse

U.S. House of Representatives Managers

INTRODUCTION

This trial arises from President Donald J. Trump's incitement of insurrection against the Republic he swore to protect. The House of Representatives has impeached him for that constitutional offense. To protect our democracy and national security—and to deter any future President who would consider provoking violence in pursuit of power—the Senate should convict President Trump and disqualify him from future federal officeholding.

On January 6, 2021, with Vice President Michael Pence presiding, Congress assembled to perform one of its most solemn constitutional responsibilities: the counting of electoral votes for President of the United States. This ritual has marked the peaceful transfer of power in the United States for centuries. Since the dawn of the Republic, no enemy—foreign or domestic—had ever obstructed Congress's counting of the votes. No President had ever refused to accept an election result or defied the lawful processes for resolving electoral disputes. Until President Trump.

In a grievous betrayal of his Oath of Office, President Trump incited a violent mob to attack the United States Capitol during the Joint Session, thus impeding Congress's confirmation of Joseph R. Biden, Jr. as the winner of the presidential election. As it stormed the Capitol, the mob yelled out "President Trump Sent Us," "Hang Mike Pence," and "Traitor Traitor Traitor." The insurrectionists assaulted police officers with weapons and chemical agents. They seized control of the Senate chamber floor, the Office of the Speaker of the House, and major sections of the Capitol complex. Members and their staffs were trapped and terrorized. Many officials (including the Vice President himself) barely escaped the rioters. The line of succession to the Presidency was endangered. Our seat of government was violated, vandalized, and desecrated. Congress's counting of electoral votes was delayed until nightfall and not completed until 4 AM. Hundreds of people were injured in the assault. Five people—including a Capitol Police officer—died.

President Trump's responsibility for the events of January 6 is unmistakable. After losing the 2020 election, President Trump refused to accept the will of the American people. He spent months asserting, without evidence, that he won in a "landslide" and that the election was "stolen." He amplified these lies at every turn, seeking to convince supporters that they were victims of a massive electoral conspiracy that threatened the Nation's continued existence. But every single court to consider the President's attacks on the outcome of the election rejected them. And state and federal officials from both parties refused President Trump's increasingly desperate demands that they break the law to keep him in power. With his options running out, President Trump announced a "Save America Rally" on January 6. He promised it would be "wild."

By the day of the rally, President Trump had spent months using his bully pulpit to insist that the Joint Session of Congress was the final act of a vast plot to destroy America. As a result—and as had been widely reported—the crowd was armed, angry, and dangerous. Before President Trump took the stage, his lawyer called for "trial by combat." His son warned Republican legislators against finalizing the election results: "We're coming for you." Finally, President Trump appeared behind a podium bearing the presidential seal. Surveying the tense crowd before him, President Trump whipped it into a frenzy, exhorting followers to "fight like hell [or] you're not going to have a country anymore." Then he aimed them straight at the Capitol, declaring: "You'll never take back our country with weakness. You have to show strength, and you have to be strong."

Incited by President Trump, his mob attacked the Capitol. This assault unfolded live on television before a horrified nation. But President Trump did not take swift action to stop the violence. Instead, while Vice President Pence and Congress fled, and while Capitol Police officers battled insurrectionists, President Trump was reportedly "delighted" by the mayhem he had unleashed, because it was preventing Congress from affirming his election loss. This dereliction of duty—this failure to take charge of a decisive security response and to quell the riotous mob—persisted late into the day. In fact, when Congressional leaders begged President Trump to send help, or to urge his supporters to stand down, he instead renewed his attacks on the Vice President and focused on lobbying Senators to challenge the election results. Only *hours* after his mob first breached the Capitol did President Trump release a video statement calling for peace—and even then, he told the insurrectionists (who were at that very moment rampaging through the Capitol) "we love you" and "you're very special." President Trump then doubled down at 6:01pm, issuing a tweet that blamed Congress for not surrendering to his demand that the election results be overturned: "These are the things and events that happen when a sacred landslide election victory is so unceremoniously & viciously stripped away from great patriots who have been badly & unfairly treated for so long. Go home with love & in peace. Remember this day forever!"

The Nation will indeed remember January 6, 2021—and President Trump's singular responsibility for that tragedy. It is impossible to imagine the events of January 6 occurring without President Trump creating a powder keg, striking a match, and then seeking personal advantage from the ensuing havoc. In the words of Representative Liz Cheney, the House Republican Conference Chair: "The President of the United States summoned this mob, assembled the mob, and lit the flame of this attack. Everything that followed was his doing. None of this would have happened without the President. The President could have immediately and forcefully intervened to stop the violence. He did not. There has never been a greater betrayal by a President of the United States of his office and his oath to the Constitution."[1] Senate Minority Leader Mitch McConnell recently affirmed that "[t]he mob was fed lies" and "provoked by the president."[2]

President Trump committed this high crime and misdemeanor amid his final days in office. Given the clarity of the evidence and the egregiousness of his wrongdoing, the House approved an article of impeachment for incitement of insurrection. Now, merely weeks later, President Trump will argue that it serves no purpose to subject him to a trial and that the Senate lacks jurisdiction to do so. He is mistaken. As we explain at length below—and as scholars from diverse viewpoints have long recognized—the text and structure of the Constitution, as well as its original meaning and prior interpretations by Congress, overwhelmingly demonstrate that a former official remains subject to trial and conviction for abuses committed in office. Any other rule would make little sense. The Constitution governs the first day of the President's term, the last day, and every moment in between. Presidents do not get a free pass to commit high crimes and misdemeanors near the end of their term. The Framers of our Constitution feared more than anything a President who would abuse power to remain in office against the will of the electorate. Allowing Presidents to subvert elections without consequence would encourage the most dangerous of abuses.

For that reason, President Trump's conduct must be declared unacceptable in the clearest and most unequivocal terms. This is not a partisan matter. His actions directly threatened the very foundation on which all other political debates and disagreements unfold. They also threatened the constitutional system that protects the fundamental freedoms we cherish. It is one thing for an official to pursue legal processes for contesting election results. It is something else entirely for that

---

[1] Liz Cheney, *I Will Vote To Impeach The President* (Jan. 12, 2021).

[2] Mike DeBonis & Paul Kane, *Uncertainty Reigns in Senate as Schumer Pushes Fast Agenda and McConnell Calls Out Trump*, Wash. Post (Jan. 19, 2021).

official to incite violence against the government, and to obstruct the finalization of election results, after judges and election officials conclude that his challenges lack proof and legal merit.

To reaffirm our core constitutional principles—and to deter future Presidents from attempting to subvert our Nation's elections—the Senate should convict President Trump and disqualify him from holding or enjoying "any Office or honor, Trust, or Profit under the United States."[3] That outcome is not only supported by the facts and the law; it is also the right thing to do. President Trump has demonstrated beyond doubt that he will resort to any method to maintain or reassert his grip on power. A President who violently attacks the democratic process has no right to participate in it. Only after President Trump is held to account for his actions can the Nation move forward with unity of purpose and commitment to the Constitution. And only then will future Presidents know that Congress stands vigilant in its defense of our democracy.

STATEMENT OF FACTS

A. President Trump Refuses to Accept the Results of the 2020 Election

Before a single voter cast a ballot in the 2020 presidential election, President Trump made it clear that he had no intention of abiding by the verdict of the American people.[4] In a July 2020 interview, he pointedly refused to agree that he would accept the election results.[5] Pressed in September 2020 on whether he would "commit to making sure that there is a peaceful transferal [sic] of power after the election," he responded: "We're going to have to see what happens."[6] Throughout this period, he insisted at rallies and through social media that if he appeared to lose the

---

[3] U.S. Const., Art. I, § 3, cl. 7.

[4] Nick Niedzwiadek, *The 9 Most Notable Comments Trump Has Made About Accepting the Election Results*, Politico (Sept. 24, 2020).

[5] Ryan Goodman et al., *Incitement Timeline: Year of Trump's Actions Leading to the Attack on the Capitol*, Just Security (Jan. 11, 2021).

[6] *Id.*

election, the only possible explanation was a conspiracy to defraud him and those who supported him. On August 17, for instance, he asserted that "the only way we're going to lose this election is if this election is rigged."[7] One week later, he declared that "[t]he only way they can take this election away from us is if this is a rigged election."[8] He echoed these points at every opportunity, laying the groundwork for a refusal to accept any outcome other than his own continued grip on power.

This was not mere rhetoric, as became apparent immediately after Election Day. Based on incomplete early returns, and despite warnings from virtually every expert and election official in the country, President Trump claimed victory and tried to stop states from counting millions of lawful ballots. On November 4, for example, he tweeted: "We are up BIG, but they are trying to STEAL the Election. We will never let them do it."[9] Over the following days, many media outlets (including Fox News) reported that Joseph R. Biden, Jr. had won the election. President Trump responded by asserting—on November 8—that "this was a stolen election."[10] He repeated that same theme many times over the following months, urging his supporters to "Stop the Steal!"[11]

It was never clear who President Trump blamed for this asserted fraud—which, according to him, was vast enough to affect the outcome in many different states. At various points throughout

---

[7] *Donald Trump Speech Transcript Wisconsin August 17*, Rev (Aug. 17, 2020).

[8] *Donald Trump 2020 RNC Speech Transcript August 24*, Rev (Aug. 24, 2020).

[9] Donald J. Trump (@realDonaldTrump), Twitter (Nov. 4, 2020, 12:49 AM).

[10] Donald J. Trump (@realDonaldTrump), Twitter (Nov. 8, 2020, 9:17 AM).

[11] *See e.g.*, Donald J. Trump (@realDonaldTrump), Twitter (Nov. 21, 2020 3:34 PM) (Watch: Hundreds of Activists Gather for 'Stop the Steal' Rally in Georgia https://t.co/vUG1bqG9yg via BreitbartNews Big Rallies all over the Country. The proof pouring in is undeniable. Many more votes than needed. This was a LANDSLIDE!"); Donald J. Trump (@realDonaldTrump), Twitter (Nov. 24, 2020 10:45 PM) ("Poll: 79 Percent of Trump Voters Believe 'Election Was Stolen' https://t.co/PmMBmt05AI via @BreitbartNews They are 100% correct, but we are fighting hard. Our big lawsuit, which spells out in great detail all of the ballot fraud and more, will soon be filled. RIGGED ELECTION!"); *Donald Trump Speech on Election Fraud Claims Transcript, December 2*, Rev (Dec. 2, 2020) (But no matter when it happens, when they see fraud, when they see false votes and when those votes number far more than is necessary, you can't let another person steal that election from you. All over the country, people are together in holding up signs, "Stop the steal."); Donald J. Trump (@realDonaldTrump), Twitter (Dec. 19, 2020 9:41 AM) (He didn't win the Election. He lost all 6 Swing States, by a lot. They then dumped hundreds of thousands of votes in each one, and got caught. Now Republican politicians have to fight so that their great victory is not stolen. Don't be weak fools!).

late 2020, President Trump accused some combination of corrupt state election officials, fraudulent voters, doctored voting machines, and unspecified shadowy actors. In a speech on December 2, for example, he alleged "tremendous voter fraud and irregularities" resulting from a suspicious late-night "massive dump" of votes; he added in this speech that certain votes were "counted in foreign countries," that "[m]illions of votes were cast illegally in the swing states alone," and that "[i]t is statistically impossible" that he lost.[12] "This election was rigged," he insisted.[13]

Our legal system affords many ways in which a candidate can contest the outcome of an election. President Trump took full advantage of those opportunities, focusing on the states in which he claimed President Biden had been improperly recognized as the winner: Arizona, Georgia, Michigan, Nevada, Pennsylvania, and Wisconsin. President Trump and his allies ultimately filed 62 lawsuits in state and federal courts contesting every aspect of those elections.[14] But all of these suits were dismissed, save for one marginal Pennsylvania suit that did not affect the outcome there.[15] In dismissing these suits, judges at all levels—including several of President Trump's own judicial appointees—found that his claims were "not credible," "without merit," and "flat out wrong."[16] Courts warned that some of his suits improperly aimed to "breed confusion," "undermine the public's trust in the election," and "ignore the will of millions of voters."[17] As Judge Stephanos Bibas (a Trump appointee) observed in one characteristic opinion: "Free, fair elections are the lifeblood of

---

[12] *Donald Trump Speech on Election Fraud Claims Transcript, December 2*, Rev (Dec. 2, 2020).

[13] *Id.*; *see also, e.g.*, Donald J. Trump (@realDonaldTrump), Twitter (Dec. 30, 2020 2:48 PM) ("United States had more votes than it had people voting, by a lot. This travesty cannot be allowed to stand. It was a Rigged Election, one not even fit for third world countries!").

[14] William Cummings et al., *By the Numbers: President Donald Trump's Failed Efforts to Overturn the Election*, USA Today (Jan. 6, 2021).

[15] *Id.*

[16] *Id.*

[17] Allison Durkee, *Trump Election Lawsuit Against Brad Raffensperger, Brian Kemp Fails in Georgia*, Forbes (Jan. 5, 2021).

our democracy. Charges of unfairness are serious. But calling an election unfair does not make it so. Charges require specific allegations and then proof. We have neither here."[18] The U.S. Supreme Court itself denied numerous emergency applications aimed at overturning the election results; in response, President Trump tweeted that our highest court is "totally incompetent and weak on the massive Election Fraud that took place in the 2020 Presidential Election."[19]

President Trump had the right to seek redress through the legal system. But he turned to improper and abusive means of staying in power when it became clear that the courts were unconvinced by his claims. Specifically, he launched a pressure campaign initially aimed at state election officials that soon expanded to the Department of Justice and Members of Congress.

Starting in mid-November, President Trump brought the full power of his office to bear on state officials, pushing them to overturn and block certification of the election results by any means necessary. He pursued this agenda through tweets, phone calls, and meetings with officials, seeking at every opportunity to reverse the election so that he could remain in office.[20] For example, despite clear evidence of President Biden's victory in Michigan, President Trump issued false accusations that "[t]he Democrats cheated big time and got caught."[21] He personally lobbied two members of the Board of Canvassers for Wayne County to rescind their prior votes in favor of certifying the election results.[22] He also (unsuccessfully) tried to induce Michigan's top Republican legislative

---

[18] *Donald J. Trump For President v. Boockvar*, No. 20-3371 (3d Cir. Nov. 27, 2020).

[19] Donald J. Trump (@realDonaldTrump), Twitter (Dec. 26, 2020 8:51 AM).

[20] Maggie Haberman et al., *Trump Targets Michigan in His Ploy to Subvert the Election*, N.Y. Times (Nov. 19, 2020); Amy Gardner et al., *Trump asks Pennsylvania House Speaker for Help Overturning Election Results, Personally Intervening in a Third State*, Wash. Post (Dec. 8, 2020); Ryan Randazzo et al., *Arizona Legislature 'Cannot and Will Not' Overturn Election, Republican House Speaker Says*, Arizona Republic (Dec. 4, 2020).

[21] Donald J. Trump (@realDonaldTrump), Twitter (Nov. 18, 2020) ("The Great State of Michigan, with votes being far greater than the number of people who voted, cannot certify the election. The Democrats cheated big time, and got caught. A Republican WIN!").

[22] Kendall Karson et al., *Republican Canvassers Ask To 'Rescind' Their Votes Certifying Michigan Election Results*, ABC News (Nov. 19, 2020).

officials to violate Michigan law by rejecting the popular vote and selecting a Trump slate of electors; in furtherance of this effort, he had them fly to Washington, D.C., for a White House meeting.[23]

Trump applied particularly intense pressure to Georgia officials. On November 11, while Georgia's vote count was in progress, Republican Secretary of State Brad Raffensperger publicly stated that there was no evidence of widespread voter fraud and that ballots were being accurately counted.[24] President Trump then tweeted about Raffensperger seventeen times between November 11 and the date on which Georgia finally certified its election results. On Thanksgiving Day, he declared Raffensperger an "enemy of the people" for insisting upon the integrity of Georgia's election.[25] Reflecting an ominous pattern that would recur many times over the weeks that followed, President Trump's attacks on Raffensperger sparked threats of death and violence; one such message warned that "the Raffenspergers should be put on trial for treason and face execution."[26] Nonetheless, President Trump continued his assault on Raffensperger. President Trump's attacks were so concerning that Gabriel Sterling, another Republican election official in Georgia, publicly warned: "Mr. President … Stop inspiring people to commit potential acts of violence. Someone's going to get hurt, someone's going to get shot, someone's going to get killed."[27]

President Trump's campaign to reverse the election results—and to keep himself in the White House—lasted through the days immediately preceding the assault on the Capitol. On

---

[23] Tom Hamburger et al., *Trump Invites Michigan Republican Leaders To Meet Him At White House As He Escalates Attempts To Overturn Election Results*, Wash. Post (Nov. 19, 2020).

[24] Tim Reid & Lisa Lambert, *Republican Georgia Secretary of State Says No Sign of Widespread Fraud in Vote Count*, Reuters (Nov. 11, 2020).

[25] Tim Kephart, *Trump Calls Ga. Secretary of State "Enemy of the People"*, CBS46 (Nov. 27, 2020).

[26] Jake Lahut, *Georgia's Republican Secretary Of State And His Wife Received Texts Telling Them They Deserve 'To Face A Firing Squad' As Trump Escalated His Attacks On Election Results*, Business Insider (Nov. 19, 2020); Donald J. Trump (@realDonaldTrump), Twitter (Dec. 7, 2020, 7:50 PM).

[27] Stephen Fowler, *'Someone's Going To Get Killed': Ga. Official Blasts GOP Silence On Election Threats*, NPR (Dec. 1, 2020).

December 23, for instance, President Trump reportedly called one of Georgia's lead election investigators, urging him to "find the fraud" and claiming that the official would be a "national hero" if he did so.[28] On January 2, President Trump called Raffensperger to push him to somehow "find" enough votes to overturn the state's results: "I just want to find 11,780 votes, which is one more than we have because we won the state."[29] President Trump also made a clear and chilling threat to Georgia's highest election official: Failing to "find" enough votes to overturn the results of the Georgia election would be "a criminal offense" and "a big risk to you."[30] By this point, it was evident that President Trump would resort to any means necessary to reverse the election outcome.

That is confirmed by his persistent (and increasingly extreme) efforts to transform DOJ into an arm of his assault on state election results. At President Trump's direction, then-Attorney General William Barr authorized federal prosecutors "to pursue substantial allegations of voting and vote tabulation irregularities prior to the certification of elections."[31] That prompted sixteen Assistant United States Attorneys in fifteen districts to urge Barr to cease the investigation because there was no evidence of such substantial voting irregularities. DOJ's own investigation ultimately confirmed as much: Barr announced on December 1 that DOJ had "uncovered no evidence of widespread voter fraud that could change the outcome of the 2020 election."[32] Barr reportedly told President Trump at the time that his claims of election stealing were "bullshit."[33]

---

[28] Amy Gardner, *'Find the Fraud': Trump Pressured a Georgia Elections Investigator in a Separate Call Legal Experts Say Could Amount to Obstruction*, Wash. Post (Jan. 9, 2021).

[29] Amy Gardner & Paulina Firozi, *Here's the Full Transcript and Audio of the Call Between Trump and Raffensperger*, Wash. Post (Jan. 5, 2021).

[30] *Id.*

[31] Katie Benner & Michael S. Schmidt, *Barr Hands Prosecutors the Authority to Investigate Voter Fraud Claims*, N.Y. Times (Nov. 9, 2020); Memorandum from the Attorney General, Post-Voting Election Irregularity Inquiries (Nov. 9, 2020).

[32] Michael Balsamo, *Disputing Trump, Barr Says No Widespread Election Fraud*, Associated Press (Dec. 1, 2020).

[33] Jesse Byrnes, *Barr Told Trump that Theories About Stolen Election Were 'Bulls---': Report*, The Hill (Jan. 18, 2021).

President Trump then apparently pressured Barr's successor, Acting Attorney General Jeffrey Rosen, to appoint special counsels and file briefs aimed at overturning the election results.[34] When Rosen refused, President Trump reportedly hatched a scheme to fire Rosen and replace him with a different official who would be willing to deploy DOJ's resources in support of President Trump's efforts to keep himself in office.[35] President Trump backed down only after he learned that most of DOJ's political leadership would resign in protest if he fired Rosen.[36]

As this timeline indicates, President Trump's rejection of the election results—and his steadily more extreme efforts to overturn them—persisted from Election Day through January 6. He did not cease his campaign even after the Electoral College met on December 14, with presidential electors casting 306 Biden votes and only 232 Trump votes. Nor did he cease after Senate Majority Leader McConnell recognized Mr. Biden's victory: "Many millions of us hoped that the presidential election would yield a different result, but our system of government has processes to determine who will be sworn in on January the 20th. The Electoral College has spoken."[37] Instead, President Trump responded to these developments by escalating and refocusing his attacks on Members of Congress, pushing them to reject the Electoral College vote and then engineer his retention in office. On December 18, for instance, he tweeted that "@senatemajldr and Republican

---

[34] Katie Benner, *Trump and Justice Dept. Lawyer Said to Have Plotted to Oust Acting Attorney General*, N.Y. Times (Jan. 22, 2021); Matt Zapotosky et al., *Trump Entertained Plan to Install an Attorney General Who Would Help Him Pursue Baseless Election Fraud Claims*, Wash. Post (Jan. 22, 2021); Jess Bravin & Sadie Gurman, *Trump Pressed Justice Department to Go Directly to Supreme Court to Overturn Election Results*, Wall Street J. (Jan. 23, 2021).

[35] *Id.*

[36] Katie Benner, *Trump and Justice Dept. Lawyer Said to Have Plotted to Oust Acting Attorney General*, N.Y. Times (Jan. 22, 2021).

[37] Niels Lesniewski, *McConnell Recognizes Biden Win: The Electoral College Has Spoken*, Roll Call (Dec. 15, 2020); Nicholas Fandos, *Defying Trump, McConnell Seeks to Squelch Bid to Overturn the Election*, N.Y. Times (Dec. 15, 2020).

Senators have to get tougher, or you won't have a Republican Party anymore. We won the Presidential Election, by a lot. FIGHT FOR IT. Don't let them take it away!"[38]

B. President Trump Encourages His Followers to Come to Washington on January 6, 2021 and "Fight" to Overturn the Election Results

Following the Electoral College vote, President Trump fixated on January 6, 2021—the date of the Joint Session of Congress—as presenting his last, best hope to reverse the election results and remain in power. Even as he continued improperly pressuring state officials, DOJ, and Members of Congress to overturn the electoral outcome, he sharply escalated his public statements, using more incendiary and violent language to urge supporters to "stop the steal" on January 6. He insisted that the election had been "rigged" and "stolen," and that his followers had to "fight like hell" and "fight to the death" against this "act of war," since they "can't let it happen" and "won't take it anymore!" These statements turned his "wild" rally on January 6 into a powder keg waiting to blow. Indeed, it was obvious and entirely foreseeable that the furious crowd assembled before President Trump at the "Save America Rally" on January 6 was primed (and prepared) for violence if he lit a spark.

By mid-December 2020, President Trump had spent months insisting to his base that the only way he could lose the election was a dangerous, wide-ranging conspiracy against them that threatened America itself. After the Electoral College vote, he channeled that fury toward January 6, which he presented as the final firewall against a historic fraud that "stole" their democracy. On December 19, he tweeted: "Statistically impossible to have lost the 2020 Election. Big protest in D.C. on January 6th. **Be there, will be wild!**"[39] On December 26, he tweeted: "If a Democrat Presidential Candidate had an Election Rigged & Stolen, with proof of such acts at a level never seen

---

[38] Donald J. Trump (@realDonaldTrump), Twitter (Dec. 18, 2020, 9:14 AM).
[39] Donald J. Trump (@realDonaldTrump), Twitter (Dec. 19, 2020, 1:42 AM).

before, the Democrat Senators would consider it an **act of war, and fight to the death.** Mitch & the Republicans do NOTHING, just want to let it pass. NO FIGHT!" (emphasis added).[40] Fourteen minutes later, he tweeted again: "The 'Justice' Department and the FBI have done nothing about the 2020 Presidential Election Voter Fraud, **the biggest SCAM in our nation's history,** despite overwhelming evidence. They should be ashamed. History will remember. **Never give up. See everyone in D.C. on January 6th**."[41] And on January 1, he tweeted: "The BIG Protest Rally in Washington, D.C., will take place at 11.00 AM on January 6th . . . **StopTheSteal!"**[42] That same day, Kylie Jane Kremer, the head of Women For America First—a group that had helped organize the Second Million MAGA March on December 12 (which ended in 4 stabbings and 33 arrests)[43]—tweeted a link to the website "Trumpmarch.com." At the top of the post she added, "the cavalry is coming Mr. President!" President Trump retweeted her post, responding, "A great honor!"[44]

As January 6 approached, and President Trump's other attempts to overturn the election failed (including his schemes at DOJ), he further escalated his call to arms. On January 4, he gave an angry speech in Dalton, Georgia, warning that "**Democrats are trying to steal the White House ... [y]ou can't let it happen. You can't let it happen,**" and "**they're not taking this White House. We're going to fight like hell, I'll tell you right now**."[45] The next day, on January 5, he tweeted: "Washington is being inundated with people who don't want to see an election victory stolen by emboldened Radical Left Democrats. Our Country has had enough, **they won't take it**

---

[40] Donald J. Trump (@realDonaldTrump), Twitter (Dec. 26, 2020, 8:00 AM).
[41] Donald J. Trump (@realDonaldTrump), Twitter (Dec. 26, 2020, 8:14 AM).
[42] Donald J. Trump (@realDonaldTrump), Twitter (Jan. 1, 2021, 2:53 PM).
[43] NBC Washington Staff, *4 Stabbed, 33 Arrested as Trump Supporters, Counterprotesters Clash in Downtown DC*, NBC Washington (Dec. 12, 2020).
[44] Donald J. Trump (@realDonaldTrump), Twitter (Jan. 1, 2021, 12:52 PM); Donald J. Trump (@realDonaldTrump), Twitter (Jan. 1, 2021, 3:34 PM).
[45] Donald Trump Rally Speech Transcript Dalton, Georgia: Senate Runoff Election, Rev (Jan. 4, 2021).

anymore! We hear you (and love you) from the Oval Office. MAKE AMERICA GREAT AGAIN!"[46] Trump made it clear that his goal was to prevent the election results from being certified: **"I hope the Democrats, and even more importantly, the weak and ineffective RINO section of the Republican Party, are looking** at the thousands of people pouring into D.C. They won't stand for a landslide election victory to be stolen. @senatemajldr @JohnCornyn @SenJohnThune"[47]

Through these and other statements, President Trump spent the weeks preceding his rally doing everything in his power to persuade attendees that their votes—and the election itself—were going to be stolen away in the Joint Session of Congress. That is, unless they somehow stopped it by making plans to "fight like hell" and "fight to the death" against this "act of war" by "Radical Left Democrats" and the "weak and ineffective RINO section of the Republican Party."

By this point, it was clear that President Trump was comfortable urging, approving, and even celebrating violence. During a debate on September 29, for instance, he told the Proud Boys—a violent extremist group with ties to white nationalism—to "stand back and stand by."[48] On October 30, when a caravan of his supporters in Texas attacked a bus full of Biden campaign workers, nearly running it off the road, President Trump tweeted a stylized video of the caravan and captioned it, "I LOVE TEXAS!"[49] Days later, he declared that "these patriots"—who could easily have killed a busload of innocent campaign staff—"did nothing wrong."[50]

---

46 Donald J. Trump (@realDonaldTrump), Twitter (Jan. 5, 2021, 5:05 PM).

47 Donald J. Trump (@realDonaldTrump), Twitter (Jan. 5, 2021, 5:12 PM).

48 Sheera Frenkel & Annie Karni, *Proud Boys Celebrate Trump's 'Stand By' Remark About Them At The Debate*, New York Times (Sept. 29, 2020).

49 Donald J. Trump (@realDonaldTrump), Twitter (Oct. 31, 2020 8:14 PM).

50 Donald J. Trump (@realDonaldTrump), Twitter (Nov. 1, 2020, 8:18 AM); Katie Shepherd, *Trump Cheers Supporters Who Swarmed A Biden Bus In Texas: 'These Patriots Did Nothing Wrong'*, Wash. Post (Nov. 2, 2020).

Throughout this period, it was widely reported and well known that President Trump's attacks on election officials had sparked threats, intimidation, and actual violence.[51] Following President Trump's attacks on Michigan's election process, armed supporters surrounded the home of the Michigan Secretary of State; after President Trump's attacks on the election in Arizona, his supporters surrounded the home of the Arizona Secretary of State and chanted, "We are watching you!"; after President Trump targeted the election outcome in Georgia, state election officials received a wave of death threats.[52] On December 1, as described above, Gabriel Sterling (who voted for Trump) warned President Trump that his incendiary rhetoric could mean that "someone's going to get killed." Yet President Trump not only refused to condemn any of this dangerous and threatening conduct; as detailed above, he also escalated his inflammatory and militaristic demands. That trend was matched by escalating violence. On December 12, for instance, clashes between Trump supporters and law enforcement and counter protestors at the "Second Million MAGA March" resulted in dozens of arrests and several stabbings, and at least one leader of the Proud Boys was later arrested for vandalizing a church.[53]

Given all that, the crowd which assembled on January 6 unsurprisingly included many who were armed, angry, and dangerous—and poised on a hair trigger for President Trump to confirm that they indeed had to "fight" to save America from an imagined conspiracy. Answering to the President's call to mobilize, thousands arrived in Washington for the purpose (aggressively

---

[51] Michael Wines, *Here Are the Threats Terrorizing Election Workers*, N.Y. Times (Dec. 3, 2020).

[52] Nick Corasaniti et al., *As Trump Rails Against Loss, His Supporters Become More Threatening*, N.Y. Times (updated Jan. 7, 2021); *Video: Group Chants 'We Are Watching You' outside Arizona Secretary of State Katie Hobbs' Home*, KPNX-TV 12 News (Nov. 18, 2020).

[53] Peter Hermann & Keith Alexander, *Proud Boys Leader Barred From District By Judge Following His Arrest*, Wash. Post (Jan. 5, 2021); Jason Slotkin et al., *4 Stabbed, 33 Arrested After Trump Supporters, Counterprotesters Clash in D.C.*, NPR (Dec. 12, 2020).

championed by the President) of doing anything necessary to stop the Joint Session of Congress from finalizing the election results. Many who arrived brought weapons, plans of the Capitol building, and even tactical gear, including ropes, military helmets, ladders, and zip tie restraints.[54]

This mobilization was not hidden away in the dead of night. It was widely discussed on websites—such as TheDonald.win—that, as confirmed by a former White House staff member, were "closely monitored" by President Trump's social media operation.[55] These sites hosted hundreds of posts about plans for the attack on the Capitol, with detailed discussions of weaponry and directions to "find the tunnels" and "arrest the worst traitors."[56] At TheDonald.win, one poster stated: "If Congress illegally certifies Biden, … Trump would have absolutely no choice but to demand us to storm Congress and kill/beat them up for it."[57] Another poster wrote: "[Trump] can order the NAT guard to stand down if needed. unfortunately he has no control over the Capitol Police... but there are only around 2k of them and a lot are useless fat asses or girls."[58] In their posts, extremists made it clear that they were prepared to fight at President Trump's direction.

These calls for violence at the Capitol were widely covered. On January 2, for example, Fox News reported on a social media declaration by Proud Boys Leader Enrique Tarrio that the Proud Boys would come to the January 6 rally prepared for violence.[59] Another Proud Boys organizer said,

---

[54] *See, e.g.*, Evan Hill et al., *They Got a Officer!': How a Mob Dragged and Beat Police at the Capitol*, N.Y. Times (Jan. 11, 2021); Peter Hermann, *'We Got to Hold This Door'*, Wash. Post (Jan. 14, 2021); Rich Schapiro, *Stun Guns, 'Stinger Whips' and a Crossbow: What Police Found on the Capitol Protesters*, NBC News (Jan. 13, 2021).

[55] Andrew Feinberg, White House Insiders Say Trump Knew What Was About To Happen At The Capitol—Because of His Social Media Guru Dan Scavino, Independent (Jan. 12, 2021).

[56] Adam Rawnsley and Justin Rohrlich, *'Ready to Die': Two Months of MAGA Mob Warning Signs*, The Daily Beast (Jan. 7, 2021).

[57] Greg Miller et al., *A Mob Insurrection Stoked by False Claims Of Election Fraud And Promises Of Violent Restoration*, Wash. Post (Jan. 9, 2021).

[58] House Judiciary Committee Majority Staff Report: Materials in Support of H. Res. 24, Impeaching Donald John Trump, President of the United States, for High Crimes and Misdemeanors, 117th Cong, at 20 (Jan. 12, 2021).

[59] Caitlin McFall, *Proud Boys Flock to Washington 'Incognito' for Jan. 6 Protests*, Fox News (Jan. 2, 2021).

"We are going to smell like you, move like you, and look like you. The only thing we'll do that's us is think like us! Jan 6th is gonna be epic."[60] On January 5, the *Washington Post* warned that "[f]ar-right online forums are seething with references to potential violence and urging supporters of President Trump to bring guns to Wednesday's protests in Washington."[61] These calls to action, the *Washington Post* explained, were "direct responses to Trump's demands that his supporters pack the nation's capital in support of his bogus claims that November's national vote for Biden resulted from election fraud."[62] Other outlets reported threats to the Joint Session, with headlines such as "Violent threats ripple through far-right internet forums ahead of protest," and "MAGA Geniuses Plot Takeover of US Capitol."[63]

City officials, such as D.C. Mayor Muriel Bowser, also warned that the rally posed a high risk of violence. Mayor Bowser announced that all D.C. police officers would report on January 6, and asked residents to avoid the downtown area and "not to engage with demonstrators who come to our city seeking confrontation."[64] Law enforcement activity in the days leading up to January 6 confirmed that the gathering was dangerous. On January 3, a Capitol Police intelligence report warned of increased risk of violence targeted against Congress "as the last opportunity to overturn the results of the presidential election."[65] On January 5, an FBI office in Virginia also issued an

---

[60] Joshua Zitser, *Far-Right Group Proud Boys Claim They Will Attend January 6 Rally 'Incognito' and Wear All-Black to Blend In With Antifa Protestors*, Business Insider (Jan. 3, 2021).

[61] Craig Timberg & Drew Harwell, *Pro-Trump Forums Erupt with Violent Threats Ahead of Wednesday's Rally Against the 2020 Election*, Wash. Post (Jan. 5, 2021).

[62] *Id.*.

[63] Brandy Zadrozny & Ben Collins, *Violent Threats Ripple Through Far-Right Internet Forums Ahead of Protest*, NBC News (Jan. 5, 2021); Andrew Beaujon, *MAGA Geniuses Plot Takeover of US Capitol*, Washingtonian (Jan. 5, 2021); Luke Barr, *Law Enforcement Braces For Protests As Trump Supporters Gather In Captial*, ABC News (Jan. 5, 2021).

[64] Press Release, Office of the Mayor of the District of Columbia, Mayor Bowser Continues Preparation for Upcoming First Amendment Demonstrations (Jan 3, 2021).

[65] Carol D. Leonnig, Capitol Police Intelligence Report Warned Three Days Before Attack That 'Congress Itself' Could Be Targeted, Washington Post (Jan. 15, 2021).

explicit warning that extremists were preparing to travel to Washington to commit violence and start a "war."[66] District of Columbia police made several protest-related arrests on January 4 and 5, including for weapons charges and assaulting a police officer. The arrests were widely publicized and included the leader of the Proud Boys, who was arrested with high capacity firearms magazines, which he claimed were meant to be supplied to another rally attendant.[67]

In all these ways—and more, as we will show at trial—President Trump created a powder keg on January 6. Hundreds were prepared for violence at his direction. They were prepared to do whatever it took to keep him in power. All they needed to hear was that their President needed them to "fight like hell." All they needed was for President Trump to strike a match.

C. Vice President Pence Refuses to Overturn the Election Results

By the time the rally began, President Trump had nearly run out of options. He had only one card left to play: his Vice President. But in an act that President Trump saw as an unforgivable betrayal, Vice President Pence refused to violate his oath and constitutional duty—and, just hours later, had to be rushed from the Senate chamber to escape an armed mob seeking vengeance.

In the weeks leading up to the rally, President Trump had furiously lobbied Vice President Pence to refuse to count electoral votes for President Biden from any of the swing states.[68] These demands ignored the reality that the Vice President has no constitutional or statutory authority to take that step. Over and over again, President Trump publicly declared that if Vice President Pence refused to block the Joint Session from finalizing President Biden's victory, then the election, the

---

[66] Devlin Barrett and Matt Zapotosky, *FBI Report Warned Of 'War' At Capitol, Contradicting Claims There Was No Indication Of Looming Violence*, Washington Post (Jan. 12, 2021).

[67] Jennifer Steinhauer et al., *Leader of Proud Boys, a Far-Right Group, Is Arrested as D.C. Braces for Protests*, N.Y. Times (Jan. 4, 2021); Peter Hermann & Keith Alexander, *Proud Boys Leader Barred From District By Judge Following His Arrest*, Wash. Post (Jan. 5, 2021).

[68] Jonathan Swan, Zachary Basu, *Off the Rails Episode 7: Trump Turns on* Pence, Axios (Jan. 20, 2021).

party, and the country would be lost. "I hope Mike Pence comes through for us, I have to tell you," President Trump said in Georgia on January 4.[69] The next day, he tweeted: "If Vice President @Mike_Pence comes through for us, we will win the Presidency."[70] President Trump reiterated this demand just hours before the rally: "States want to correct their votes, which they now know were based on irregularities and fraud, plus corrupt process never received legislative approval. All Mike Pence has to do is send them back to the States, AND WE WIN. Do it Mike, this is a time for extreme courage!"[71] On the morning of January 6, President Trump reportedly told Vice President Pence, "You can either go down in history as a patriot, or you can go down in history as a pussy."[72]

Later that day, while President Trump was speaking at his rally, Vice President Pence issued a public letter rejecting President Trump's threats. "It is my considered judgment," he wrote, "that my oath to support and defend the Constitution constrains me from claiming unilateral authority to determine which electoral votes should be counted and which should not."[73]

This letter sounded the death knell to any peaceful methods of overturning the election outcome. It was well known that the House and Senate were going to count the lawfully certified electoral votes they had received. President Trump's efforts to coerce election officials, state legislatures, the DOJ, Members of Congress, and his own Vice President had all failed. But he had long made it clear that he would *never* accept defeat. He would fight until the bitter end. And all that remained for President Trump was the seething crowd before him—known to be poised for

---

[69] Donald Trump Rally Speech Transcript Dalton, Georgia: Senate Runoff Election, Rev (Jan. 4, 2021).
[70] Donald J. Trump (@realDonaldTrump), Twitter (Jan. 6, 2021, 1:00 AM).
[71] Donald J. Trump (@realDonaldTrump), Twitter (Jan. 6, 2021, 8:17 AM).
[72] Peter Baker et al., *Pence Reached His Limit With Trump. It Wasn't Pretty.*, N.Y. Times (Jan. 12, 2021).
[73] Mike Pence (@Mike_Pence), Twitter (Jan. 6, 2021, 1:02 PM).

violence at his instigation—and the Capitol building just a short march away, where Vice President Pence presided over the final, definitive accounting of President Trump's electoral loss.

D. President Trump Incites Insurrectionists to Attack the Capitol

Shortly before noon on January 6, President Trump took the stage at his "Save America Rally" and spoke from a podium bearing the Seal of the President of the United States.[74] By the time he addressed the angry crowd, Rudy Giuliani (his lawyer) had called for "trial by combat."[75] President Trump praised Giuliani, saying "he's got guts, he fights."

Over the following hour, President Trump repeatedly reiterated his claim that Democrats had "stolen" the election. He described vote tranches that favored President Biden as "explosions of bullshit."[76] He exhorted the crowd to "**fight much harder**" to "**stop the steal**" and "**take back our country**."[77] He also demanded again that Vice President Pence illegally interfere with the work of the Joint Session—a position that the Vice President rejected even as President Trump spoke. Time and again, President Trump declared that the future of the country was on the line and that only the crowd assembled before him could stop the massive fraud taking place at the Capitol.

At numerous points during the rally, President Trump urged the crowd toward the Capitol, where the Joint Session was about to start.[78] In response, an early wave surged toward the building and started to pull down barricades around its perimeter. Twenty minutes into the rally, President Trump said that those marching toward the Capitol should do so "peacefully." But then he spoke

---

[74] *Watch LIVE: Save America March at The Ellipse featuring President @realDonaldTrump*, RSBN TV (Jan. 6, 2020).

[75] *Id.*; *see also Rudy Giuliani Speech Transcript at Trump's Washington, D.C. Rally: Wants 'Trial by Combat'*, Rev (Jan. 6, 2021).

[76] *Watch LIVE: Save America March at The Ellipse featuring President @realDonaldTrump*, RSBN TV (Jan. 6, 2020).

[77] *Id.*; *see also* Maggie Haberman, *Trump Told Crowd 'You Will Never Take Back Our Country with Weakness'*, N.Y. Times (Jan. 6, 2021).

[78] *Watch LIVE:* Save *America March at The Ellipse featuring President @realDonaldTrump*, RSBN TV (Jan. 6, 2020).

for another 50 minutes, using highly inflammatory rhetoric—exactly the kind of language calculated to incite violence given what had been reported about the crowd. He declared, "**we fight, we fight like hell**," because "**if you don't fight like hell you're not going to have a country anymore**."[79]

Videos of the crowd eliminate any doubt that President Trump's words *in fact* incited the crowd to commit violence. Immediately after President Trump told the crowd that "**you'll never take back our country with weakness**," and that "**[y]ou have to show strength**," supporters can be heard loudly shouting "take the Capitol right now!" and "invade the Capitol building!"[80] At another point, the crowd interrupted him with chants of "Fight for Trump!" The President did not try to soothe their aggression, but instead smiled and responded, "Thank you."[81] As many in the crowd instantly recognized, the tenor of his speech (and his repeated demand that they "fight like hell" and "show strength" to save their country) belied any desire for a peaceful demonstration.[82] Those who had come to the rally looking for a signal from their President found it in his remarks. Rather than quell the crowd, urge peaceful demonstration, or promise to carry on the fight over the years to come, the overwhelming thrust of President Trump's remarks—delivered to an armed, angry crowd widely known to be prepared for violence on his behalf—was a militaristic demand that they must fight to stop what was occurring in the Capitol at that very moment.

President Trump ended his speech by again imploring supporters to march to the Capitol, shouting, "So let's walk down Pennsylvania Avenue!"[83] Although President Trump ducked out and

---

[79] *Id.*

[80] Ryan Goodman & Justin Hendrix, *"Fight for Trump": Video Evidence of Incitement at the Capitol*, Just Security (Jan. 25, 2021).

[81] *Watch LIVE:* Save *America March at The Ellipse featuring President @realDonaldTrump*, RSBN TV (Jan. 6, 2020).

[82] Julia Jacobo, *This Is What Trump Told Supporters before Many Stormed Capitol Hill*, ABC News (Jan. 7, 2021).

[83] *Id.*

returned to the White House to watch the day's events on television—and to lobby allies to stall the Joint Session—thousands of people, many of them armed, marched on the Capitol as he instructed.

E. Insurrectionists Incited by President Trump Attack the Capitol

Provoked and incited by President Trump, who told them to "fight like hell," hundreds of insurrectionists arrived at the Capitol and launched an assault on the building—a seditious, deadly attack against the Legislative Branch and the Vice President without parallel in American history.

In short order, President Trump's mob crashed through security barriers that had been set up around the Capitol perimeter, tore down scaffolding, and bludgeoned law enforcement personnel guarding the building.[84] Rioters wearing Trump paraphernalia shoved and punched Capitol Police officers, gouged their eyes, assaulted them with pepper spray and projectiles, and denounced them as "cowards" and "traitors."[85] Rioters attacked law enforcement personnel with weapons they had brought with them or stolen from the police: sledgehammers, baseball bats, hockey sticks, crutches, flagpoles, police shields, and fire extinguishers.[86] They tore off officers' helmets, beat them with batons, and deployed chemical irritants including bear spray, a chemical irritant similar to tear gas, designed to be used by hunters to fend off bear attacks.[87] Some attackers wore gas masks and bulletproof vests; many carried firearms—indeed, at least six handguns were recovered after the

---

[84] Lauren Leatherby et al., *How a Presidential Rally Turned Into a Capitol Rampage*, N.Y. Times (Jan. 12, 2021).

[85] Marc Fisher et al., *The Four-Hour Insurrection*, Wash. Post (Jan. 7, 2021).

[86] Evan Hill et al., *They Got a Officer!': How a Mob Dragged and Beat Police at the Capitol*, N.Y. Times (Jan. 11, 2021); Peter Hermann, *'We Got to Hold This Door'*, Wash. Post (Jan. 14, 2021).

[87] *Id.*; Peter Hermann, *'We Got to Hold This Door'*, Wash. Post (Jan. 14, 2021); Lauren Leatherby et al., *How a Presidential Rally Turned Into a Capitol Rampage*, N.Y. Times (Jan. 12, 2021); Rich Schapiro, *Stun Guns, 'Stinger Whips' and a Crossbow: What Police Found on the Capitol Protesters*, NBC News (Jan. 13, 2021).

insurrection[88]—while others carried knives, brass knuckles, a noose, and other deadly weapons.[89] One officer attempting to guard the Capitol described the attack as a "medieval battle scene."[90]

After storming through the barricades surrounding the building, rioters laid siege to the Capitol itself. One rioter screamed, "What are we waiting for? We already voted and what have they done? They stole it! We want our fucking country back! Let's take it!"[91] Some in the mob scaled walls to reach the Capitol, while others climbed makeshift ladders and still others clambered over one another to get inside.[92] The mob physically overwhelmed law enforcement personnel guarding the entrances to the building and smashed through windows to gain access.[93] Police put their own lives at risk to defend the Capitol, but they were overcome by a crush of insurrectionists.

The mob breached the Capitol on the Senate side first, after the Joint Session had separated for each Chamber to consider an objection to Arizona's Electoral College votes.[94] Senators were in the midst of debate when rioters stormed into the building.[95] Secret Service agents swiftly rushed Vice President Pence out of the Senate and evacuated him and his family to elsewhere in the Capitol complex, avoiding a potentially deadly encounter.[96] A Capitol Police officer shrewdly and heroically led a violent crowd away from the entrance to the Senate Chamber, narrowly preventing a swarm of

---

[88] *See, e.g.*, Officer Dallan Haynes Statement of Facts, at 2 (Jan. 7, 2021); DC Police Department (@DCPoliceDept), Twitter (Jan. 7, 2021, 1:52 PM).

[89] Officer Christopher Frank Affidavit, at 1 (Jan. 6, 2021), https://perma.cc/YN87-BDKH; Officer Alexandria Sims Affidavit, at 1 (Jan. 7, 2021), https://perma.cc/392C-CGPC; Special Agent Lawrence Anyaso Affidavit, at 1 (Jan. 7, 2021), https://perma.cc/M3GZ-WSVM; Luke Mogelson, *Among the Insurrectionists*, The New Yorker (Jan. 15, 2021).

[90] Peter Hermann, *'We Got to Hold This Door'*, Wash. Post (Jan. 14, 2021).

[91] Ryan Goodman & Justin Hendrix, *'Fight for Trump': Video Evidence of Incitement at the Capitol*, Just Security (Jan. 25, 2021).

[92] Marc Fisher et al., *The Four-Hour Insurrection*, Wash. Post (Jan. 7, 2021).

[93] *Id.*

[94] Lauren Leatherby & Anjali Singhvi, *Critical Moments in the Capitol Siege*, N.Y. Times (Jan. 15, 2021).

[95] Lauren Leatherby et al., *How a Presidential Rally Turned Into a Capitol Rampage*, N.Y. Times (Jan. 12, 2021).

[96] Ashley Parker et al., *How the Rioters Who Stormed the Capitol Came Dangerously Close to Pence*, Wash. Post (Jan. 15, 2021).

insurrectionists from overcoming Senators who remained just feet away.[97] After that, the violent mob inside the Capitol embarked on a deadly mission.

Videos of the events show that dozens of the insurrectionists specifically hunted Vice President Pence and House Speaker Nancy Pelosi—the first and second in the line of Presidential succession, respectively. "Once we found out Pence turned on us and that they had stolen the election, like, officially, the crowd went crazy," said one rioter. "I mean, it became a mob."[98] Rioters chanted, "**Hang Mike Pence!**"[99] Another shouted, "Mike Pence, we're coming for you … fucking traitor!"[100] Others shouted, "**Tell Pelosi we're coming for that bitch**."[101] One rioter said that he and other rioters "kicked in Nancy Pelosi's office door" and that "Crazy Nancy probably would have been torn into little pieces but she was nowhere to be seen."[102]

The insurrectionists also menaced Members of Congress, their staffs, their families, and Capitol personnel. Senators were evacuated from their Chamber, scrambling quickly just as the mob massed nearby.[103] Rioters ultimately overpowered Capitol Police throughout the complex, forcing them to retreat closer and closer to where Members had sought safety. In the House, terrified Members were trapped in the Chamber; they prayed and tried to build makeshift defenses while

---

[97] *Id.*; Rebecca Tan, *A Black Officer Faced Down a Mostly White Mob at the Capitol. Meet Eugene Goodman*, Wash. Post (Jan. 14, 2021).

[98] Ashley Parker et al., *How the Rioters Who Stormed the Capitol Came Dangerously Close to Pence*, Wash. Post (Jan. 15, 2021).

[99] Peter Baker et al., *Pence Reached His Limit with Trump. It Wasn't Pretty*, N.Y. Times (Jan. 12, 2021).

[100] Ryan Goodman & Justin Hendrix, *'Fight for Trump': Video Evidence of Incitement at the Capitol*, Just Security (Jan. 25, 2021).

[101] Matthew S. Schwartz, *As Inauguration Nears, Concern Of More Violence Grows*, NPR (Jan. 9, 2021).

[102] David K. Li & Ali Gostanian, *Georgia Lawyer Said He Kicked in Pelosi's Door. She Could've Been 'Torn into Little Pieces'*, NBC News (Jan. 19, 2021).

[103] Marc Fisher et al., *The Four-Hour Insurrection*, Wash. Post (Jan. 7, 2021).

rioters smashed the entryway.[104] Capitol Police dragged furniture to barricade the House Chamber doors against the mob attempting to break in; they then drew their guns to guard the doors.[105] Instructed to put on gas masks to protect against chemical agents, some Members called loved ones for fear that they would not survive the assault by President Trump's insurrectionist mob.[106]

As Members on the House floor evacuated through the Speaker's Lobby, rioters saw them and attempted to break through the barricaded glass door, which Capitol Police protected with their guns drawn. The officer at the door shot one woman attempting to break through, merely ten yards from the path where Members were being evacuated to safety from the House floor. Meanwhile, Members of Congress, press, and staff remained trapped in the Gallery, one floor up and fearing for their lives. When gunshots were heard outside the House Chamber, police screamed, "Get down! Get down!" and Members in the Gallery crawled to shelter behind chairs.[107]

Members and staff who were not on the House floor at the time of the siege were also in danger. Many barricaded themselves in their offices. Speaker Pelosi's staff hid under a table with the lights turned off for hours while they could hear rioters outside in the Speaker's office.[108] One Member asked his chief of staff to protect his visiting daughter and son-in-law "with her life"—which she did by standing guard at the door clutching a fire iron while his family hid under a table.[109]

---

[104] Lauren Leatherby et al., *How a Presidential Rally Turned Into a Capitol Rampage*, N.Y. Times (Jan. 12, 2021); CBS News, *Video Shows Members of Congress Taking Cover in House Gallery* (Jan. 6, 2021); Haley Britzky, *This Army Ranger-Turned-Congressman Was Last Out of the House Chamber During the Capitol Riots*, Task and Purpose (Jan. 7, 2021).

[105] CNN, *Lawmaker Describes Moment Captured in Dramatic Photo*, YouTube (Jan. 6, 2021).

[106] Rep. Dan Killdee (@RepDanKildee), Twitter, (Jan. 6, 2021, 2:52 PM); Rose Minutaglio, *Rep. Susan Wild On The 'Sheer Panic' She Felt In That Viral Photo*, Elle (Jan. 7, 2021).

[107] Rose Minutaglio, *Rep. Susan Wild On The 'Sheer Panic' She Felt In That Viral Photo*, Elle (Jan. 7, 2021).

[108] Christina Zhao, *Pelosi Gets Emotional Talking About Her Staffers Hiding Under Desks Amid Capitol Riot*, Newsweek (Jan. 10, 2021).

[109] John Hendrickson, *Jamie Raskin Lost His Son. Then He Fled a Mob*, The Atlantic (Jan. 8, 2021).

Once inside, insurrectionists desecrated and vandalized the Capitol. They ransacked Congressional Leadership offices—breaking windows and furniture, and stealing electronics and other sensitive material.[110] They left bullet marks in the walls, looted art, smeared feces in hallways, and destroyed monuments, including a commemorative display honoring the late Representative John Lewis.[111] Many rioters carried Trump flags and signs, while others wore the insignia of fringe militias and extremists such as the Proud Boys and neo-Nazis, including a shirt emblazoned with the slogan, "Camp Auschwitz."[112] One insurrectionist paraded the Confederate battle flag through the Capitol halls—an act that thousands of troops gave their lives to prevent during the Civil War.[113]

Shortly after Senators had been evacuated from the Senate Chamber, insurrectionists entered it and rummaged through Senators' desks, taking photos of private notes and letters.[114] One of them shouted "Trump won that election!" on the Senate dais where Vice President Pence had presided.[115] Another rioter climbed onto the dais, announcing that "I'm gonna take a seat in this chair, because Mike Pence is a fucking traitor."[116] He left a note on the Vice President's desk stating, "ITS ONLY

---

[110] Natasha Bertrand, *Justice Department Warns of National Security Fallout from Capitol Hill Insurrection*, Politico (Jan. 7, 2021); Wilson Wong, *Shattered Glass, Ransacked Offices: Images of Damage at U.S. Capitol Left by Pro-Trump Mob*, NBC News (Jan. 7, 2021).

[111] *See* Chris Sommerfeldt, *Pro-Trump Rioters Smeared Poop in U.S. Capitol Hallways During Belligerent Attack*, N.Y. Daily News (Jan. 7, 2021); The Hill (@thehill), Twitter (Jan. 7, 2021, 1:16 PM); Sarah Bahr, *Curators Scour Capitol for Damage to the Building or Its Art*, N.Y. Times (Jan. 7, 2021); Lauren Egan, *Capitol Reels from Damage and Destruction Left by Violent Rioters*, NBC News (Jan. 7, 2021).

[112] *Here Are Some of the People Charged since a Mob Breached the Capitol*, Wash. Post (Jan. 15, 2021); Elana Schor, *Anti-Semitism Seen in Capitol Insurrection Raises Alarms*, Associated Press (Jan. 13, 2021); Special Agent Affidavit, at 13 (Jan. 15, 2021), https://www.justice.gov/opa/page/file/1355921/download.

[113] *Id.*; Julia Jacobo, *A Visual Timeline on How the Attack on Capitol Hill Unfolded*, ABC News (Jan. 10, 2021).

[114] *Id.*; Lauren Leatherby & Anjali Singhvi, *Critical Moments in the Capitol Siege*, N.Y. Times (Jan. 15, 2021); Luke Mogelson, *Among the Insurrectionists*, The New Yorker (Jan. 15, 2021).

[115] Igor Bobic (@igorbobic), Twitter (Jan. 6, 2021, 2:47 PM).

[116] Luke Mogelson, *Among the Insurrectionists*, The New Yorker (Jan 15. 2021).

A MATTER OF TIME / JUSTICE IS COMING."[117] Some insurrectionists carried zip ties that could be used as handcuffs—apparently in anticipation of taking hostages.[118]

Meanwhile, the mob outside the building continued to attack the police and wreak havoc. Some erected a gallows directly outside of the Capitol.[119] Others disabled police vehicles, and still others left threatening messages for Members of Congress.[120] In a nearby pickup truck belonging to a Trump supporter who had driven to Washington for the day's events, police discovered materials for making napalm-like explosives, a rifle, a shotgun, three pistols, five types of ammunition, a crossbow, several machetes, a stun gun, and smoke devices.[121] Police found two other explosive devices near the Capitol, outside the offices of the Republican National Committee and the Democratic National Committee.[122] Law enforcement is currently seeking more information on a hooded figure captured on camera transporting the suspected pipe bombs.[123]

Provoked by President Trump's statements at the rally, many insurrectionists who assaulted the Capitol proudly proclaimed that they were doing President Trump's bidding. One told police officers that he came as part of a group of "patriots" "at the request of the President."[124] In a livestreamed video from inside the Capitol, another declared that "**[o]ur president wants us here.**

---

117 *Id.*

118 Alexander Mallin & Ivan Pereira, *Capitol Riot Suspects Who Allegedly Brought Zip Ties, Wore Tactical Gear Arrested*, ABC News (Jan. 11, 2021).

119 Azi Paybarah & Brent Lewis, *Stunning Images as a Mob Storms the U.S. Capitol*, N.Y. Times (Jan. 6, 2021).

120 *Id.*

121 *Here Are Some of the People Charged Since a Mob Breached the Capitol*, Wash. Post (Jan. 15, 2021).

122 Michael Balsamo, *Discovery of Pipe Bombs in DC Obscured by Riot at Capitol*, Associated Press (Jan. 11, 2021).

123 *See* DC Police Department (@DCPoliceDept), Twitter (Jan. 8, 2021, 10:52 AM).

124 Special Agent James Soltes Affidavit, at 3 (Jan. 8, 2021).

... We wait and take orders from our president."[125] Yet another rioter yelled at police officers, **"[w]e were invited here ... by the President of the United States!"**[126]

After the insurrection, one participant who broke into the Capitol wearing combat gear and carrying zip ties stated that he acted because "[t]he President asked for his supporters to be there to attend, and I felt like it was important, because of how much I love this country, to actually be there."[127] Another asserted, "I thought I was following my President. ... He asked us to fly there, he asked us to be there, so **I was doing what he asked us to do**."[128] She explained that she believed that she had "**answered the call of [her] president**," echoing the views of other participants.[129] Subsequent reporting revealed that far-right groups had rallied members to attend the event based upon "the green light from the President."[130]

The insurrectionists killed a Capitol Police officer by striking him in the head with a fire extinguisher.[131] They injured over 140 police officers, including at least 81 U.S. Capitol Police officers and 65 members of the Metropolitan Police Department, with many requiring hospitalization and significant medical treatment.[132] One suffered an apparent heart attack after he was hit six times with a stun gun; another lost part of a finger.[133] To cite just a few of the many

---

[125] Dan Barry et al., *'Our President Wants Us Here': The Mob That Stormed the Capitol*, N.Y. Times (Jan. 9, 2021).

[126] *See* Philip Bump, *A House Republican Wanted Proof of Incitement. Here Are Four Rioters Who Came to D.C. Because of Trump*, Wash. Post (Jan. 13, 2021).

[127] *Here Are Some of the People Charged since a Mob Breached the Capitol*, Wash. Post (Jan. 15, 2021).

[128] David Begnaud (@DavidBegnaud), Twitter (Jan. 15, 2021, 8:30 PM).

[129] Alan Feurer & Nicole Hong, *'I Answered the Call of My President': Rioters Say Trump Urged Them On*, N.Y. Times (Jan. 17, 2021).

[130] Georgia Wells et al., *Proud Boys, Seizing Trump's Call to Washington, Helped Lead Capitol Attack*, Wall Street J. (Jan. 17, 2021); Aruna Viswanatha & Sadie Gurman, *Far-Right Affiliations Seen among Those Recently Charged in Capitol Riot*, Wall Street J. (Jan. 17, 2021).

[131] Marc Santora et al., *Capitol Police Officer Dies from Injuries in Pro-Trump Rampage*, N.Y. Times (Jan. 8, 2021).

[132] Peter Hermann & Julie Zauzmer, *Beaten, Sprayed with Mace and Hit with Stun Guns: Police Describe Injuries to Dozens of Officers during Assault on U.S. Capitol*, Wash. Post (Jan. 11, 2021); Special Agent Michael Palian Affidavit, at 5 (Jan. 19, 2021); Tom Jackman, *Police Union Says 140 Officers Injured in Capitol Riot*, Wash. Post (Jan. 27, 2021).

[133] Peter Hermann & Julie Zauzmer, *Beaten, Sprayed with Mace and Hit with Stun Guns: Police Describe Injuries to Dozens of Officers during Assault on U.S. Capitol*, Wash. Post (Jan. 11, 2021).

incidents of violence captured on video: multiple officers were dragged down a flight of stairs and beaten with metal pipes and an American flag pole; another was bludgeoned with a hockey stick; another was crushed as he attempted to guard a door to the Capitol.[134] Rioters shouted as they surrounded one fallen officer: "We got one!" Others urged, "Kill him with his own gun!"[135] Four rioters died during the attack.[136]

It took more than three hours to secure the Capitol after the insurrectionists invaded the building.[137] Another three hours passed before the Joint Session could resume.[138] The rioters tried but—as Majority Leader McConnell noted—ultimately failed to prevent Vice President Pence and Congress from carrying out their constitutional responsibility to count the Electoral College votes.[139] At approximately 4 AM, President Biden was confirmed as the winner of the 2020 election.[140]

F. President Trump's Dereliction of Duty During the Attack

As armed insurrectionists breached the Capitol—and as Vice President Pence, the Congress, and the Capitol Police feared for their lives—President Trump was described by those around him as "borderline enthusiastic because it meant the certification was being derailed."[141] Senior administration officials described President Trump as "delighted" and reported that he was "walking around the White House confused about why other people on his team weren't as excited as he was

---

[134] *Id.*; Evan Hill et al., *They Got a Officer!': How a Mob Dragged and Beat Police at the Capitol*, N.Y. Times (Jan. 11, 2021); Katie Shepherd, *Video Shows Capitol Mob Dragging Police Officer Down Stairs. One Rioter Beat the Officer with a Pole Flying the U.S. Flag*, Wash. Post (Jan. 11, 2021); Peter Hermann, *'We Got to Hold This Door'*, Wash. Post (Jan. 14, 2021); Pierre Thomas et al., *'Like a Medieval Battle Scene": Officers Recount Being Attacked by Capitol Mob*, ABC News (Jan. 15, 2021).

[135] Peter Hermann, *'We Got to Hold This Door'*, Wash. Post (Jan. 14, 2021).

[136] Jack Healy, *These Are the Five People Who Died in the Capitol Riot*, New York Times (Jan. 11, 2021).

[137] Shelly Tan et al., *How One of America's Ugliest Days Unraveled Inside and Outside the Capitol*, Wash. Post (Jan. 9, 2021).

[138] *Id.*

[139] Matthew Choi, *'They Failed": McConnell Condemns Rioters Who Stormed the Capitol*, Politico (Jan. 6, 2021).

[140] Shelly Tan et al., *How One of America's Ugliest Days Unraveled Inside and Outside the Capitol*, Wash. Post (Jan. 9, 2021).

[141] Kaitlan Collins (@kaitlancollins), Twitter (Jan. 6, 2021, 10:34 PM).

as you had rioters pushing against Capitol Police trying to get into the building."[142] These feelings were reflected in President Trump's actions (and inactions) over the following hours, which reveal an extraordinary, unprecedented repudiation of the President's duties to protect the government.

At 1:49 PM, after insurrectionists had overcome the Capitol perimeter—and after reports of pipe bombs had been confirmed—President Trump retweeted a video of his speech at the rally, which included his message that "Our country has had enough, we will not take it anymore, and that's what this is all about. … You have to be strong."[143] Just over thirty minutes later, at 2:24 PM, while rioters were still attacking police and after Vice President Pence had been evacuated from the Senate floor, President Trump again tweeted to excoriate the Vice President for refusing to obstruct the Joint Session: "**Mike Pence didn't have the courage to do what should have been done to protect our Country and our Constitution**."[144] President Trump thus singled out Vice President Pence for direct criticism *at the very same time* the Vice President and his family were hiding from a violent mob provoked by President Trump. As one rioter explained, the mob "went crazy" after learning that "Pence turned on us and that they had stolen the election."[145]

As the assault continued, President Trump continued his efforts to prevent the Joint Session from affirming the election results. After Senators had been evacuated from the Senate Chamber, President Trump called Senator Mike Lee—apparently trying to reach Senator Tommy Tuberville—not to check on his safety, or assess the security threat, but to try to persuade him to delay and

---

142 Andrew Prokop, *Republican Senator: White House Aides Say Trump Was "Delighted" as Capitol Was Stormed*, Vox (Jan. 8, 2021).

143 Donald J. Trump (@realDonaldTrump), Twitter (Jan. 6, 2021, 1:49:54 PM).

144 Donald J. Trump (@realDonaldTrump), Twitter (Jan. 6, 2021, 2:24 PM).

145 Ashley Parker et al., *How the Rioters Who Stormed the Capitol Came Dangerously Close to Pence*, Wash. Post (Jan. 15, 2021).

further obstruct the Electoral College vote count.[146] In fact, there is no evidence that President Trump called Vice President Pence, Speaker Pelosi or Senator Chuck Grassley—the first three in the line of succession—or anyone else in the Capitol to check on their safety during the attack.

Recognizing President Trump's singular responsibility for the assault, as well as his unique ability to both provoke and quell the riotous mob, Members of the House and Senate from both parties urged the President to intervene.[147] This occurred both publicly and privately. House Minority Leader Kevin McCarthy confirmed that he had "talked to the President" on the telephone and said: "I think we need to make a statement. Make sure that we can calm individuals down."[148] Republican Representative Mike Gallagher tweeted, "Mr. President. You have got to stop this. You are the only person who can call this off."[149] Mick Mulvaney, the President's former Acting Chief of Staff, tweeted that President Trump "can stop this now and needs to do exactly that. Tell these folks to go home."[150] Even the President's own Chief of Staff, Mark Meadows, was prompted to speak to him after aides bluntly insisted on it: "They are going to kill people."[151]

But the President did not take any action at all in response to the attack until 2:38 PM, when he issued his first tweet, and 3:13 PM, when he issued a second. These tweets told his followers to "support our Capitol Police and Law Enforcement … Stay peaceful!"[152] and "ask[ed] everyone at the

---

146 Sunlen Serfaty et al., *As Riot Raged at Capitol, Trump Tried to Call Senators to Overturn Election*, CNN (Jan. 8, 2021).

147 *See e.g.*, Ashley Parker et al., *Six Hours of Paralysis: Inside Trump's Failure to Act after a Mob Stormed the Capitol*, Wash. Post (Jan. 11, 2021); Nancy Pelosi (@SpeakerPelosi), Twitter (Jan. 6, 2021, 3:55 PM).

148 Associated Press, *Trump Doesn't Ask Backers to Disperse after Storming Capitol*, PBS (Jan. 6, 2021); *see also Chris Christie says Trump Should Tell Protesters to Leave Capitol*, ABC News (Jan. 6, 2021).

149 Editorial, *Mike Gallagher Is Right: 'Call It Off, Mr. President'*, Wisconsin State Journal (Jan. 6, 2021).

150 Mick Mulvaney (@MickMulvaney), Twitter (Jan. 6, 2021, 3:01 PM).

151 Ashley Parker et al., *Six Hours of Paralysis: Inside Trump's Failure to Act after a Mob Stormed the Capitol*, Wash. Post (Jan. 11, 2021).

152 Donald J. Trump (@realDonaldTrump), Twitter (Jan. 6, 2021, 2:38 PM).

U.S. Capitol to remain peaceful. No violence! Remember, WE are the Party of Law & Order."[153] These tweets were, obviously, totally ineffectual at stopping the violence. And they did not reflect any substantial effort on the part of the President of the United States to protect the Congress.

During this time, not only did President Trump fail to issue unequivocal statements ordering the insurrectionists to leave the Capitol; he also failed in his duties as Commander in Chief by not immediately taking action to protect Congress and the Capitol. This failure occurred despite multiple members of Congress, from both parties, including on national television, vehemently urging President Trump to take immediate action.

The next action that President Trump took—while the violence persisted and escalated—occurred more **than three hours** from the start of the siege. At this point, he released a scripted video that included a call for "peace" and "law and order," and instructed his followers, "you have to go home now."[154] But even in that video, President Trump continued to provoke violence, telling his supporters—who were *at that very moment* committing violence inside the Capitol and terrorizing Members of Congress—that the election was "stolen from us."[155] He added that "[i]t was a landslide election and everyone knows it, especially the other side." He concluded by telling the violent insurrectionists: **"We love you, you're very special. … I know how you feel.** But go home and go home in peace."[156]

---

153 Donald J. Trump (@realDonaldTrump), Twitter (Jan. 6, 2021, 3:13 PM).

154 Donald J. Trump (@realDonaldTrump), Twitter (Jan. 6, 2021, 4:17 PM); *President Trump Video Statement on Capitol Protestors*, C-SPAN (Jan. 6, 2021).

155 *Id.*

156 *Id.*; *see also* Tony Keith, *Twitter 'Locks' President Trump for 12 Hours Wednesday Evening*, KKTV (Jan. 6, 2021).

The violence he had provoked unsurprisingly continued after President Trump released this video.[157] In the early evening, after the Capitol had finally been secured and the scope of the devastation was clear, President Trump sent another tweet. But rather than forcefully denounce the violence and express concern for the safety of law enforcement personnel and Members of Congress, he again validated the insurrection, reiterated his falsehoods about the election, and lionized the rioters as patriots: **"These are the things and events that happen when a sacred landslide election victory is so unceremoniously & viciously stripped away from great patriots who have been badly & unfairly treated for so long. Go home with love & in peace. Remember this day forever!"**[158]

Like his predecessors, President Trump swore an oath to "preserve, protect, and defend the Constitution of the United States." But on January 6, after inciting violence against the Congress to block certification of the election results, President Trump failed to honor that oath. And he concluded the day not by apologizing, or by repudiating the insurrectionists, but instead by embracing them and lending the imprimatur of the Presidency to their acts of domestic violence.

Since the events of January 6, President Trump has shown no remorse for his role in provoking an attack on our seat of government. To the contrary, he insisted to reporters days later that his speech prior to the insurrection had been "totally appropriate."[159] Despite repeated

---

[157] Evan Hill & Arielle Ray, *Body Camera Footage Shows Capitol Rioters Trampling Over Woman*, N.Y. Times (Jan. 28, 2021).

[158] Donald J. Trump (@realDonaldTrump), Twitter (Jan. 6, 2021, 6:01 PM).

[159] Kevin Liptak & Betsy Klein, *Defiant Trump Denounces Violence but Takes No Responsibility for Inciting Deadly Riot*, CNN (Jan. 12, 2021).

entreaties, it took him three days to order the flag of the United States to be flown at half-staff to commemorate the death of a Capitol Police Officer who had been killed by insurrectionists.[160]

President Trump's conduct on and after January 6 exacerbated the continuing threat of violence following the assault on the Capitol. As a result, the federal and state governments had to take unprecedented measures to ensure security in Washington. The states sent 25,000 National Guard troops to protect the inauguration of an incoming President from potential violence incited by the outgoing President.[161] In addition, state capitols across the Nation shut their doors and took extreme security measures during the days leading up to the inauguration for fear of further violence in support of President Trump.[162] As the Director of the FBI stated, there was a major "potential for violence at multiple protests and rallies" both in Washington and at state capitols around the country "that could bring armed individuals within close proximity to government buildings and officials."[163] Ultimately, President Trump announced he would not attend the inauguration of President Biden.[164] He never issued any statement condemning threatened attacks on the inauguration or repudiating violence against the lawful government of the United States of America

G. The House Approves An Article of Impeachment with Bipartisan Support

In light of the crisis that President Trump created and the overwhelming public evidence of his guilt, the House acted quickly to impeach him.[165] Five days after the assault on the Capitol, an article of impeachment for incitement of insurrection was introduced in the House and referred to

---

160 David Choi, *Trump Lowers the White House Flag after Pressure from Both Republicans and Democrats*, Business Insider (Jan. 10, 2021).

161 Emily Davies et al., *With Mall, Bridges and Streets Closed in D.C., the Nation Prepares for a Celebration of Democracy Mostly Devoid of its Citizens*, Wash. Post (Jan. 15, 2021), https://perma.cc/FR4Y-6G7N.

162 Associated Press, *State Capitols Boarded Up, Fenced Off, Patrolled by Troops*, KNAU (Jan. 18, 2021).

163 Press Release, FBI, *FBI Director Christopher Wray's Remarks at Briefing on Inauguration Security* (Jan. 15, 2021).

164 Kaitlin Collins & Kevin Liptak, *Trump Tweets He is Skipping Biden's Inauguration*, CNN (Jan. 8, 2021).

165 H. Res. 24, 117th Cong. (Jan. 11, 2021).

the House Committee on the Judiciary. The following day, the House Committee on Rules convened a hearing to take testimony on the impeachment resolution.[166] During this hearing, the Chairman of the Judiciary Committee submitted a 50-page report documenting the Committee's findings in support of impeachment.[167] At the conclusion of this hearing, the Rules Committee adopted by a recorded vote a special rule providing for House debate on the resolution.[168]

One day later—January 13, 2021—the House voted to impeach President Trump with bipartisan support on charges that he incited an insurrection. The article of impeachment was adopted with the support of 232 House Members, including every Democrat and ten Republicans.[169] The House acted with urgency because President Trump's rhetoric and conduct before, during, and after the riot made clear that he was a menace to the Nation's security and democratic system. Moreover, President Trump never disputed the facts that gave rise to his impeachment, which were captured on recordings. Instead he merely stated publicly that what he did was appropriate.

Several Republican Members of the House issued statements explaining their decision to vote for impeachment. For example, Representative John Katko explained:

> It cannot be ignored that President Trump encouraged this insurrection—both on social media ahead of January 6th, and in his speech that day. By deliberately promoting baseless theories suggesting the election was somehow stolen, the president created a combustible environment of misinformation, disenfranchisement, and division. When this manifested in violent acts on January 6th, he refused to promptly and forcefully call it off, putting countless lives in danger.[170]

---

166 *House Rules Committee Debate on Resolution to Remove President Trump From Office*, C-SPAN (Jan. 12, 2021).

167 *House Judiciary Committee Majority Staff Report: Materials in Support of H. Res. 24, Impeaching Donald John Trump, President of the United States, for High Crimes and Misdemeanors*, 117th Cong (Jan. 12, 2021).

168 U.S. House Committee on Rules, *Report on Providing for Consideration of the Resolution (H. Res. 24, Impeaching Donald John Trump, President of the United States, for High Crimes and Misdemeanors)*, H. Rept. 117-2, 117th Cong. (Jan. 12, 2021).

169 Clerk of the U.S. House of Representatives, Roll Call 17, H. Res. 24 (Jan. 13, 2021.

170 Press Release, Representative John Katko, Statement from Rep. Katko on Articles of Impeachment (Jan. 12, 2021).

Representative Tom Rice stated:

> It has been a week since so many were injured, the United States Capitol was ransacked, and six people were killed, including two police officers. Yet, the President has not addressed the nation to ask for calm. He has not visited the injured and grieving. He has not offered condolences. Yesterday in a press briefing at the border, he said his comments were "perfectly appropriate."[171]

Representative Adam Kinzinger similarly explained: "There is no doubt in my mind that the President of the United States broke his oath of office and incited this insurrection. He used his position in the Executive to attack the Legislative."[172] Representative Liz Cheney put the point simply when she recognized that "[t]here has never been a greater betrayal by a President of the United States of his office and his oath to the Constitution."[173]

ARGUMENT

I. President Trump Committed High Crimes and Misdemeanors

A President is subject to impeachment, conviction, and disqualification from future federal officeholding if he commits high crimes and misdemeanors. President Trump's incitement of insurrection meets that standard.[174] His conduct endangered the foundation of our government.

---

[171] Press Release, Representative Tom Rice, Rep. Tom Rice Votes to Impeach President Trump (Jan. 13, 2021).

[172] Press Release, Representative Adam Kinzinger, Congressman Kinzinger Statement on Impeachment (Jan. 12, 2012).

[173] Press Release, Representative Liz Cheney, I Will Vote To Impeach The President (Jan. 12, 2021).

[174] *See* Dan McLaughlin, *Convict and Disqualify Trump*, National Review (Jan. 15, 2021); David Post, *A Senatorial Impeachment Two-Step?*, The Volokh Conspiracy (Jan. 13, 2021); Gene Healy, *Only Impeachment is Censure Enough*, CATO Institute (Jan 13. 2021); Eric Posner, *The Effort to Disqualify Trump is Worth It*, Project Syndicate (Jan. 12, 2021); *ACLU Again Calls for Impeachment of President Trump*, ACLU Press Release (Jan. 10, 2021); Frank O. Bowman, III, *The Constitutional Case for Impeaching Donald Trump (Again)*, Just Security (Jan. 9, 2021); Jeannie Suk Gerson, *The Case For Removing Donald Trump*, New Yorker (Jan. 9, 2021); Michael Stokes Paulsen, *The Constitutional and Moral Imperative of Immediate Impeachment*, The Bulwark (Jan. 8, 2021); Jonathan H. Adler, *Yes, Congress May Impeach and Remove President Trump for Inciting Lawless Behavior at the Capitol*, The Volokh Conspiracy (Jan. 8, 2021); Noah Feldman, *I Testified at Trump's Last Impeachment. Impeach Him Again.*, Bloomberg (Jan. 7, 2021); Steven G. Calabresi & Norman Eisen, *We Disagree on a Lot. But We Both Think Trump Should Be Convicted*, N.Y. Times (Jan. 13, 2021); David Landau and Rosalind Dixon, *The 25th Amendment Can Remove Trump, but We Shouldn't Stop There*, N. Y. Times (Jan. 7, 2021); *Stanford Law's Michael McConnell on the 25th Amendment and Trump*,

A. President Trump Violated His Oath of Office

Every President swears an oath to "faithfully execute the Office of the President of the United States"[175] and assumes the constitutional duty to "take Care that the laws be faithfully executed."[176] Impeachment is a safeguard against Presidents who violate that oath (and betray that duty) by using the powers of their office to advance their own personal political interests at the expense of the Nation. In particular, the Framers of the Constitution feared a President who would corrupt his office by sparing "no efforts or means whatever to get himself re-elected."[177]

President Trump's effort to extend his grip on power by fomenting violence against Congress was a profound violation of the oath he swore. If provoking an insurrectionary riot against a Joint Session of Congress after losing an election is not an impeachable offense, it is hard to imagine what would be. The Framers themselves would not have hesitated to convict on these facts. Their worldview was shaped by a study of classical history, as well as a lived experience of resistance and revolution. They were well aware of the danger posed by opportunists who incited mobs to violence for political gain. They drafted the Constitution to avoid such thuggery, which they associated with "the threat of civil disorder and the early assumption of power by a dictator."[178] James Madison thus worked "to avoid the fate of those 'ancient and modern confederacies,' which he believed had succumbed to rule by demagogues and mobs."[179] The *Federalist Papers*, too, strongly

---

Stanford Law School (Jan. 7, 2021); Keith E. Whittington, *The Conservative Case For Impeaching Trump Now*, Wash. Post (Jan. 7, 2021); David Priess & Jack Goldsmith, *Can Trump Be Stopped?*, Lawfare (Jan. 7, 2021); Cass Sunstein, *Does the 25th Amendment Apply to Trump? Quite Possibly*, Bloomberg (Jan. 7, 2021); John Podhoretz, *Donald Trump Should Be Impeached and Removed from Office Tomorrow*, Commentary Magazine (Jan. 6, 2021); Melissa De Witte and Sharon Driscoll, *Stanford Scholars React to Capitol Hill Takeover*, Stanford News (Jan. 6, 2021); Ilya Somin, *A Qualified Defense of Impeaching Trump Again*, Reason (Jan. 6, 2021); Will Baude, Samuel Bray & Stephen Sachs, *Impeach and Remove*, The Volokh Conspiracy (Jan. 6, 2021).

175 U.S. Const., Art. II, § 1, cl. 8.

176 U.S. Const., Art. II, §§ 1, 3.

177 2 *The Records of the Federal Convention of 1787*, at 64 (Max Farrand ed., 1911) (Farrand).

178 Bernard Bailyn, *The Ideological Origins of the American Revolution* 282 (1967).

179 Jeffrey Rosen, *American is Living James Madison's Nightmare*, The Atlantic (October 2018).

warned against aspiring tyrants who would aggrandize themselves—and threaten the Republic—by stirring popular fury to advance personal ambition.[180] The founding generation was familiar with leaders who provoked mobs for their personal gain and threatened the political order. They would have immediately recognized President Trump's conduct on January 6 as an impeachable offense.

B. President Trump Attacked the Democratic Process

The gravity of President Trump's offense is magnified by the fact that it arose from a course of conduct aimed at subverting and obstructing the election results. Since President George Washington willingly relinquished his office after serving two terms, our Nation has seen an unbroken chain of peaceful transitions from one presidential administration to the next—that is, until January 6, 2021. President Trump's incitement of insurrection disrupted the Joint Session of Congress as it performed its duty under the Twelfth Amendment to count the Electoral College votes.[181] Although this assault was put down after several hours, and the Joint Session fulfilled its responsibility later that night, President Trump's abuse of office threatened and injured our democratic order. Under absolutely no circumstance may a candidate for any position, at any level of government, respond to electoral defeat by provoking armed violence.

As evidenced by the statements of William Davie, George Mason, and Gouverneur Morris at the Constitutional Convention, the Framers "anticipated impeachment if a President placed his own interest in retaining power above the national interest in free and fair elections."[182] At a time when "democratic self-government existed almost nowhere on earth,"[183] the Framers imagined a society "where the true principles of representation are understood and practised, and where all authority

---

[180] Alexander Hamilton, *The Federalist Papers*: No. 1.
[181] U.S. Const. Amend. XII.; Electoral Count Act of 1887, Pub. L. 49-90, 24 Stat. 373.
[182] *See* H. Rep. 116-346 at 52.
[183] Akhil Amar, *America's Constitution: A Biography* 8 (2006)

flows from, and returns at stated periods to, the people."[184] That would be possible only if "those entrusted with [power] should be kept in dependence on the people."[185] Thus, "[w]hen the President concludes that elections threaten his continued grasp on power, and therefore seeks to corrupt or interfere with them, he denies the very premise of our constitutional system."[186] President Trump placed his own political ambition above our Nation's commitment to democracy and the rule of law—and for that reason his actions plainly rank as high crimes and misdemeanors.

C. President Trump Imperiled Congress

President Trump's conduct not only harmed democracy, but also jeopardized the safety of the Vice President and nearly the entire Legislative Branch, as well as the police officers protecting the Capitol. Members of Congress and their staffs were forced to improvise barricades and hiding places while they awaited rescue by law enforcement. Others were trapped in the House Chamber, where they seized gas masks and ducked behind furniture to avoid insurrectionists. Many feared for their lives as armed attackers battered doors and Capitol Police drew weapons. The duration and severity of this threat were amplified by President Trump's dereliction of duty during the attack.

The Framers understood that "[t]he accumulation of all powers, legislative, executive, and judiciary, in the same hands, … may justly be pronounced the very definition of tyranny."[187] They wrote a Constitution that creates a system of checks and balances within the federal government. A President may be impeached for conduct that severely undermines this structural separation of powers.[188] Our constitutional system simply cannot function if the President, acting to extend his

---

[184] *See* 4 Elliot, *Debates in the Several State Conventions* at 331.
[185] James Madison, Federalist No. 37.
[186] *See* H. Rep. 116-346 at 53.
[187] James Madison, *The Federalist Papers*: No. 47.
[188] *See* H. Rept. 116-346 at 45-46, 145-148.

own grasp on power against the expressed will of the people, prompts an armed attack against a co-equal branch that prevents it from performing its core constitutional responsibilities.

President Trump's conduct will have other lasting effects on Congress. Before January 6, the Capitol was a place that the people of the United States could freely visit to see their democratic system at work. Since January 6, the Capitol complex has more closely resembled a fortress, ringed by fences with barbed wire and heavily guarded by the Capitol Police and the National Guard. The American people cannot now get anywhere near their Capitol. That is a sorry state of affairs for our Nation, one that no President should have played a role in bringing about.

D. President Trump Undermined National Security

A final consideration requiring President Trump's conviction is the harm he inflicted on the national security of the United States. Most immediately, the insurrectionist mob had access to, and stole, sensitive materials and electronics—including a laptop from the office of the Speaker of the House.[189] The U.S. Attorney for the District of Columbia has stated that "electronic items" and other "[d]ocuments [and] materials" were "stolen from [S]enators' offices."[190] These devices could be used to infiltrate federal networks.[191] It has therefore been necessary to undertake a thorough review to determine the extent of the security breach and implement appropriate remedial measures.

The attack that President Trump provoked has also emboldened other violent extremists.[192] As government officials and outside experts have warned, it may come to be seen as a rallying point for further insurrection—and as a "significant driver of violence" that inspires extremists "to engage

---

189 Raphael Satter, *Laptop Stolen from Pelosi's Office during Storming of U.S. Capitol, Says Aide*, Reuters (Jan. 8, 2021).

190 Brian Fung, *Capitol Riots Raise Urgent Concerns about Congress's Information Security*, CNN (Jan. 8, 2021).

191 Samantha Masunaga, *The Attack on the Capitol May Pose a Cybersecurity Risk. Here's How*, L.A. Times (Jan. 8, 2021).

192 Molly Hennessy-Fiske, *'Second Revolution Begins': Armed Right-Wing Groups Celebrate Capitol Attack*, L.A. Times (Jan. 6, 2021).

in more sporadic, lone-actor or small-cell violence" against targets including "racial, ethnic, or religious minorities and institutions, law enforcement, and government officials and buildings."[193] President Trump's conduct on January 6 brought distinct extremist groups into ad hoc coalition with one another, which might strengthen their "willingness, capability, and motivation to attack and undermine" the government.[194] Further, the armed insurrection has been nothing short of a "propaganda coup … in fueling recruitment and violence for years to come."[195] President Trump only made matters worse when he tweeted, in the evening, "Remember this day forever!"—a statement that armed extremists will indeed remember. (Sadly, it will be remembered too by the Members of Congress, their staffs, and the law enforcement officials who were attacked by the insurrectionist mob.) In all of these respects, President Trump made Americans less safe, particularly Americans who belong to communities targeted by right-wing extremist groups.

Finally, President Trump's conduct tarnished the reputation of the United States abroad. Images of insurrectionists sacking the seat of American democracy—stirred to action by a President who said "we love you" during the assault—have been a propaganda bonanza for America's adversaries, for whom "the sight of the U.S. Capitol shrouded in smoke and besieged by a mob whipped up by their unwillingly outgoing president" is "proof of the fallibility of Western democracy."[196] This country's reputation as a stable democracy has sustained a heavy blow. For

---

[193] Zolan Kanno-Youngs, *Federal Authorities Warn That the Capitol Breach Will Be a 'Significant Driver of Violence'*, N.Y. Times (Jan. 13, 2021).

[194] *Id.*

[195] Neil MacFarquhar et al., *Capitol Attack Could Fuel Extremist Recruitment for Years, Experts Warn*, N.Y. Times (Jan. 16, 2021).

[196] Alexander Smith & Saphora Smith, *U.S. Foes like China and Iran See Opportunity in the Chaos of Trump-Stoked Riot at Capitol*, NBC News (Jan. 8, 2021).

years to come, the insurrectionist attack that President Trump incited may gravely undermine American efforts to promote democracy, even as it emboldens authoritarian regimes.

Since our Nation was founded, it has been well recognized that impeachment is warranted for "betrayal of the Nation's interest—and especially for betrayal of national security."[197] President Trump's pursuit of power at all costs is a betrayal of historic proportions. It requires his conviction.

II. THERE IS NO DEFENSE FOR PRESIDENT TRUMP'S CONDUCT

Every argument that may be raised in President Trump's defense further demonstrates that he is a danger to our democratic system of government.

A. Fair Impeachment Process

President Trump incited a mob that attacked Congress during the Joint Session. The House's expeditious response to this attack was both necessary and appropriate. There must be no doubt that Congress will act decisively in the fact of such extraordinary abuse—which threatened not only the peaceful transfer of power, but also the very lives of senior government officials.

Any claim that the House moved too quickly in responding to a violent insurrection that President Trump incited is mistaken. The House serves as a grand jury and prosecutor under the Constitution. The events that form the basis for President Trump's impeachment occurred in plain view. They are well known to the American people. Many Members of Congress were themselves witnesses to his conduct and its consequences. There is no basis on which President Trump could assert that what a horrified Nation saw with its own eyes, and heard with its own ears, is somehow "fake news." Accordingly, in this unprecedented circumstance, the House acted squarely within its constitutional responsibilities in swiftly and emphatically approving an article of impeachment.

---

[197] H. Rept. 116-346 at 49.

Here, in the Senate, is where the Constitution calls for a trial and where President Trump will have ample opportunity to make his case through procedures that the Senate adopts.

For that reason, any process-based objections to this impeachment are wrong. This case does not involve secretive conduct, or a hidden conspiracy, requiring months or years of investigation. It does not raise complicated legal questions about the definition of a high crime and misdemeanor. And the gravity of the President's abuse—as well as the continuing nature of the threat it poses to our democracy if left unanswered—demand the clearest of responses from the Legislative Branch. Indeed, hundreds of people have already been arrested and charged for their role in the events of January 6. There is no reason for Congress to delay in holding accountable the President who incited the violent attack, inflamed the mob even as it ransacked the Capitol, and failed to take charge of a swift law enforcement response because he believed such dereliction of duty might advance his political interest in overturning the results of an election that he lost.

B. Criminality

The Constitution authorizes impeachment and conviction for "high Crimes and Misdemeanors." As Alexander Hamilton explained in the *Federalist Papers*, impeachable offenses "are of a nature which may with peculiar propriety be denominated POLITICAL, as they relate chiefly to injuries done immediately to the society itself."[198] Therefore, whether President Trump's conduct violated the criminal law is a question for prosecutors and courts; "offenses against the Constitution are different than offenses against the criminal code."[199] The only question here is

---

[198] Alexander Hamilton, *The Federalist Papers*: No. 65; *see* H. Rept. 116-346 at 58.

[199] *See* Constitutional Grounds for Presidential Impeachment, Report by the Majority Staff of the House Committee on the Judiciary, at 5 (Dec. 2019).

whether President Trump committed offenses justifying conviction and disqualification from future officeholding. For the reasons given above, the answer to that question is indisputably "yes."

C. Election Results

President Trump may persist in asserting that he actually won the 2020 presidential election, despite the overwhelming evidence to the contrary—and despite the rejection of this claim by every court and election official to consider it. President Trump may also suggest that his abuse of office is somehow justified or excused by his belief that the election was "rigged." Any such argument would rest upon demonstrable falsehoods about the legitimacy of the election results.

Moreover, we live in a Nation governed by the rule of law, not mob violence incited by candidates who cannot accept their own defeat. President Trump was not the first Presidential candidate who declared himself cheated out of victory.[200] Andrew Jackson, for instance, strongly believed that the 1824 election had been stolen from him because powerful forces refused to accept his candidacy on behalf of the common man. Richard Nixon believed in 1960 that he had been cheated out of the Presidency by widespread voter fraud in Illinois, which he thought secured John F. Kennedy's victory. And in 2000, Vice President Al Gore and many of his political supporters thought he would have won the Presidency had all of Florida's votes been properly counted. Yet despite their feelings of grievance, all of these Presidential candidates accepted the election results and acquiesced to the peaceful transfer of power required by the Constitution. President Trump, alone in our Nation's history, did not. His belief that he won the election—regardless of its truth or falsity (though it is assuredly false)—is no defense at all for his abuse of office.

---

[200] For the discussion in this paragraph, see generally Robert Mitchell, *A Presidential Election History Lesson: Americans Often Waited Days Or Weeks For The Outcome*, Wash. Post (Nov. 4, 2020).

D. Free Speech

The First Amendment exists to protect our democratic system. It supports the right to vote and ensures robust public debate. But rights of speech and political participation mean little if the President can provoke lawless action if he loses at the polls. President Trump's incitement of deadly violence to interfere with the peaceful transfer of power, and to overturn the results of the election, was therefore a direct assault on core First Amendment principles. Holding him accountable through conviction on the article of impeachment would *vindicate* First Amendment freedoms—which certainly offer no excuse or defense for President Trump's destructive conduct.

Most fundamentally, the First Amendment protects private citizens from the government; it does not protect government officials from accountability for their own abuses in office. Therefore, as scholars from across the political spectrum have recognized, the First Amendment does not apply *at all* to an impeachment proceeding.[201] The question in this case is not whether to inflict liability or punishment on a private citizen; instead, the Senate must decide whether to safeguard the Nation's constitutional order by disqualifying an official who committed egregious misconduct. As one scholar writes, "the First Amendment does not shrink the scope of the impeachment power or alter what conduct would fall within the terms of high and misdemeanors."[202]

Indeed, the notion that a President can attack our democracy, provoke violence, and interfere with the Electoral College so long as he does so through statements advocating such lawlessness would have astonished the Framers. They wrote the impeachment provisions of the

---

[201] *See* Michael C. Dorf, *Free Speech, Due Process, and Other Constitutional Limits in Senate Impeachment Trials*, Dorf on Law (Jan. 20, 2021, 7:00 AM); Keith E. Whittington, *Is There A Free Speech Defense to an Impeachment?*, Lawfare (Jan. 19, 2021, 4:18 PM); Jonathan H. Adler, *Yes, Congress May Impeach and Remove President Trump for Inciting Lawless Behavior at the Capitol*, The Volokh Conspiracy (Jan. 8, 2021, 3:21 PM); Ilya Somin, *The First Amendment Doesn't Protect Trump Against Impeachment for his Role in Inciting the Assault on the Capitol*, The Volokh Conspiracy (Jan. 8, 2021, 4:17 PM);

[202] *See* Keith E. Whittington, *Is There A Free Speech Defense to an Impeachment?*, Lawfare (Jan. 19, 2021, 4:18 PM).

Constitution to guard against *any* presidential conduct that constitutes a great and dangerous offense against the Nation—no matter the means for carrying out that malfeasance. And here, the House approved an article of impeachment that concerns not solely the President's incitement, but also his conduct preceding and following his provocation of an armed assault on the Capitol.

Regardless, even if the First Amendment were applicable here, private citizens and government officials stand on *very* different footing when it comes to being held responsible for their statements. As the leader of the Nation, the President occupies a position of unique power. And the Supreme Court has made clear that the First Amendment does not shield public officials who occupy sensitive policymaking positions from adverse actions when their speech undermines important government interests.[203] Thus, just as a President may legitimately demand the resignation of a Cabinet Secretary who publicly disagrees with him on a matter of policy (which President Trump did repeatedly), the public's elected representatives may disqualify the President from federal office when they recognize that his public statements constitute a violation of his oath of office and a high crime against the constitutional order. No one would seriously suggest that a President should be immunized from impeachment if he publicly championed the adoption of totalitarian government, swore an oath of eternal loyalty to a foreign power, or advocated that states secede from and overthrow the Union—even though private citizens could be protected by the First Amendment for such speech.[204] By its own terms, and in light of its fundamentally democratic

---

[203] *See Branti v. Finkel*, 445 U.S. 507, 517-518 (1980); *Elrod v. Burns*, 427 U.S. 347, 366-367 (1976) (plurality).

[204] *See* Keith E. Whittington, *Is There A Free Speech Defense to an Impeachment?*, Lawfare (Jan. 19, 2021, 4:18 PM) (listing additional examples).

purposes, the First Amendment does not constrain Congress from removing an official whose expression makes him unfit to hold or ever again occupy federal office.[205]

Yet even if President Trump's acts while occupying our highest office were treated like the acts of a private citizen, and even if the First Amendment somehow limited Congress's power to respond to presidential abuses, a First Amendment defense would *still* fail. Speech is not protected where it is "directed to inciting or producing imminent lawless action and is likely to incite or produce such action."[206] Given the tense, angry, and armed mob before him, President Trump's speech—in which he stated "you'll never take back our country with weakness," proclaimed that "[y]ou have to show strength," and exhorted his supporters to "go to the Capitol" and "fight like Hell" immediately before they stormed the Capitol—plainly satisfies that standard.

Separate from these legal points, President Trump may assert that this impeachment reflects "cancel culture" or some supposed intolerance of his right to voice objections to the election results. That would be a red herring. President Trump endangered the very constitutional system that protects all other rights, including freedom of expression. It would be perverse to suggest that our shared commitment to free speech requires the Senate to ignore the obvious: that President Trump is singularly responsible for the violence and destruction that unfolded in our seat of government on January 6. "It can't be that the solemn price for protecting our civil liberties against current and future abuses is that the president can incite a mob bearing huge flags with his name on them to storm the Capitol, kill a police officer, and further, not immediately tell them to stop or, as

---

[205] *Branti*, 445 U.S. at 517, 519. Indeed, impeachment is fundamentally an employment action against a public official, and thus the First Amendment would not insulate the President's statements from discipline even if it applied, because the government's interest in orderly operation would outweigh the President's speech interests. *See Garcetti v. Ceballos*, 547 U.S. 410 (2006); *Connick v. Meyers*, 461 U.S. 138 (1983); *Pickering v. Board of Education*, 391 U.S. 563 (1968).

[206] *Brandenburg v. Ohio*, 395 U.S. 444, 447 (1969).

commander-in-chief, to refuse to send help . . . . [T]hat would be a sure way to make a mockery of the civil liberties . . . contemplated and secured by the Constitution and Bill of Rights."[207]

III. The Senate Has Jurisdiction To Try This Impeachment

Given the overwhelming strength of the case against him, we expect President Trump will seek to escape any reckoning for his constitutional offenses by asserting that the Senate lacks jurisdiction over him as a former official. That argument is wrong. It is also dangerous. The period in which we hold elections and accomplish the peaceful transfer of power is a source of great pride in our nation. But the transition between administrations is also a precarious, fragile time for any democracy—ours' included. The Framers anticipated these risks and emphasized that presidential abuse aimed at our democratic process itself was the single most urgent basis for impeachment. It is unthinkable that those same Framers left us virtually defenseless against a president's treachery in his final days, allowing him to misuse power, violate his Oath, and incite insurrection against Congress and our electoral institutions simply because he is a lame duck. There is no "January Exception" to impeachment or any other provision of the Constitution. A president must answer comprehensively for his conduct in office from his first day in office through his last. Former President John Quincy Adams thus declared, "I hold myself, so long as I have the breath of life in my body, amenable to impeachment by [the] House for everything I did during the time I held any public office."[208]

As the Senate itself concluded in the trial of Secretary of War William Belknap, and as nearly every legal expert has affirmed, President Adams had the right idea. The Constitution does not allow officials to escape responsibility for committing impeachable offenses by resigning when

---

[207] Jonathan Zittrain, *Impeachment Defense, the Constitution, and Bill of Rights*, Just Security (Jan. 13, 2021).
[208] Cong. Globe, 29th Cong., 1st Sess. 641 (1846) (statement of Rep. Adams).

caught, or by waiting until the end of their term to abuse power, or by concealing misconduct until their service concludes. Experts from across the ideological spectrum, including a co-founder of the Federalist Society and Ronald Reagan's Solicitor General, agree that "[t]he Constitution's text and structure, history, and precedent make clear that Congress's impeachment power permits it to impeach, try, convict, and disqualify former officers, including former presidents."[209] Even Professor Jonathan Turley (who seems to have changed his long-held views on the subject less than a month ago) previously argued that impeaching former presidents for abuses in office is authorized by the Constitution and can serve as "a reaffirmation of the principle that, within this system, 'no man in no circumstance, can escape the account, which he owes to the laws of his country.'"[210]

It is particularly obvious that the Senate has jurisdiction here because President Trump was in office at the time he was impeached. There can be no doubt that the House had authority to impeach him at that point. So the question is not whether a former official can ever be impeached by the House—though, as we will explain, this is indeed authorized. The only issue actually presented is whether the Senate has jurisdiction to conduct a trial of *this* impeachment. And Article I, Section 3, Clause 6 provides a straightforward answer to that question: "The Senate shall have the sole Power to try *all* Impeachments" (emphasis added). As Professor Michael McConnell, a former Court of Appeals judge appointed by President George W. Bush, explains: "The key word is 'all.' This clause contains no reservation or limitation. It does not say 'the Senate has power to try

---

[209] *See* Constitutional Law Scholars on Impeaching Former Officers (Jan. 21, 2021), available at https://www.politico.com/f/?id=00000177-2646-de27-a5f7-3fe714ac0000; *see also* Congressional Research Service, *The Impeachment and Trial of a Former President* 1-2 (Jan. 15, 2021) ("[I]t appears that most scholars who have closely examined the question have concluded that Congress has authority to extend the impeachment process to officials who are no longer in office.").

[210] Jonathan Turley, *Senate Trials and Factional Disputes: Impeachment As A Madisonian Device*, 49 Duke L.J. 1, 96 (1999); *see also* Jonathan Turley, *The Executive Function Theory, the Hamilton Affair, and Other Constitutional Mythologies*, 77 N.C. L. Rev. 1791, 1827 (1999).

impeachments against sitting officers.' Given that the impeachment of Mr. Trump was legitimate, the text makes clear that the Senate has power to try that impeachment."[211]

Accordingly, the Senate should not turn aside from centuries of its own practice and understanding. President Trump is personally responsible for inciting an armed attack on our seat of government that imperiled the lives of the Vice President, Members of Congress and our families, and those who staff and serve the Legislative Branch. The Nation cannot simply "move on" from presidential incitement of insurrection. If the Senate does not try President Trump (and convict him) it risks declaring to all future Presidents that there will be no consequences, no accountability, indeed no Congressional response at all if they violate their Oath to "preserve, protect and defend the Constitution" in their final weeks—and instead provoke lethal violence in a lawless effort to retain power. That precedent would horrify the Framers, who wrote the Presidential Oath of Office into the Constitution and attached no January Exception to it. President Trump must therefore stand trial for his high crimes and misdemeanors against the American people.

A. Former Officials in England and the Early American States Were Subject to Impeachment and Disqualification for Abuses Committed in Office

As revolutionaries who overthrew a king, the Framers obsessed over protecting their young Republic from the abuse of power. Based on the history of impeachment in England and the early American states, they would have considered it self-evident that a former official like President Trump could be impeached and tried for high crimes and demeanors he had committed in office.

---

[211] Quoted in Eugene Volokh, *Impeaching Officials While They're in Office, but Trying Them After They Leave*, The Volokh Conspiracy (Jan. 28, 2021), https://reason.com/volokh/2021/01/28/impeaching-officials-while-theyre-in-office-but-trying-them-after-they-leave/

When the Framers gathered in Philadelphia in 1787, they did not invent the impeachment power from scratch. As Alexander Hamilton explained in Federalist No. 65, they looked to English history, which provided "the model from which the idea of this institution has been borrowed."[212] The Framers were also influenced by "several of the State constitutions."[213] *Id.* And it was firmly established in both England and the early states that former officials were subject to impeachment for abuses in office. This was not a remotely controversial view. It was widely accepted. By vesting Congress with the power of "impeachment," the Framers incorporated that history and meaning.

Looking to the unwritten British constitution confirms that former officials were subject to impeachment. In fact, "Parliament impeached only two men during the 18th century, both former officers."[214] In 1725, former Lord Chancellor Macclesfield was impeached and convicted for acts of bribery committed during his tenure in office.[215] And while the Framers deliberated in Philadelphia in 1787, they knew that Warren Hastings faced charges in Parliament arising from abuses he had committed as the former Governor General of Bengal.[216] Those charges were championed by no less a figure than Edmund Burke, a great and founding figure of conservative political theory.

Early American states followed English practice in this respect. The impeachment of former officials was thus "known and accepted" under early state constitutions.[217] Five states—including Virginia and Pennsylvania—specifically authorized such impeachments.[218] In some states, *only* former officials (not current officials) could be impeached, which confirms the centrality of the

---

[212] *The Federalist No. 65*, at 397 (Alexander Hamilton) (Clinton Rossiter ed., 1961).

[213] *Id.*

[214] Keith Whittington, *Yes, the Senate Can Try Trump*, Wall Street Journal (Jan. 22, 2021).

[215] *See* Brian C. Kalt, *The Constitutional Case for the Impeachability of Former Federal Officials: An Analysis of the Law, History, and Practice of Late Impeachment*, 6 Tex. Rev. L. & Pol. 13, 26 (2001) (hereinafter, *Former Officials*).

[216] *See id.* at 26-27.

[217] *Id.* at 27.

[218] *Id.* at 29-31.

disqualification remedy to early American thinking about impeachment and the oddity of any suggestion that former officials can never be impeached.[219] Looking to the state constitutions that allowed impeachment but did not expressly address former officials confirms that impeaching former officials was indeed consistent with American legal traditions.[220] And no state constitution expressly prohibited such impeachments.[221] Moreover, the precept that former officials could be impeached was acted upon: in 1781, for instance, the Virginia General Assembly subjected Thomas Jefferson to an impeachment inquiry after he completed his term as governor.[222]

As defined by British and early American practice, the phrase "impeachment" was thus understood as covering former officials. That was the rule on both sides of the Atlantic. Prohibiting former official impeachments would have been a marked departure from common legal usage and tradition—the kind of departure that we might expect to trigger heated debates and considerable writing. But as explained below, there were no such debates and there were no such writings. If anything, the Framers' deliberations confirm adherence to the tradition they inherited.

Throughout this early period, disqualification was recognized as essential to achieving the core purposes of impeachment. "Especially in an age of long, varied careers, it was very significant that an impeachment conviction said not only 'get out!' but added an emphatic and irreversible 'and stay out!'"[223] Removal alone was not enough to protect the public from corrupt and abusive officials, who might later seek reelection or reappointment—and whose misconduct could create dangerous precedents if not decisively repudiated. Disqualification gave teeth to impeachment. The

---

[219] *See id.*
[220] *See id.* at 34-35.
[221] *See id.*
[222] *See id.* at 29.
[223] *Id.* at 73-74.

threat of disqualification deterred officials from abusing their power by reminding them that "their political existence depends upon their good behavior."[224] It allowed legislatures to convene inquests—and to hold public trials—that "served as a vehicle for exposing and formally condemning official wrongdoing, or for a former officeholder to clear his name."[225] Finally, it protected society from those who dishonored their offices and might do so again, whenever their abuse of power may have occurred or been discovered. These purposes defined the impeachment power as it was known to the Framers, who wrote it into the Constitution as a safeguard against presidential abuse.

B. The Framers Adhered to the Tradition That Former Officials Were Subject to Impeachment, Conviction, and Disqualification for Misconduct in Office

The records of the Constitutional Convention and a close study of the Constitution's text confirm that a former official like President Trump remains subject to impeachment and trial for high crimes and misdemeanors. History, originalism, and textualism thus leave no doubt that the Senate has jurisdiction—and a constitutional duty—to decide this case on the merits.

As Justice Robert Jackson wisely observed, "the purpose of the Constitution was not only to grant power, but to keep it from getting out of hand."[226] Nowhere is that truer than with regard to the presidency. As Edmund Randolph warned, "the Executive will have great opportunitys of abusing his power."[227] Impeachment was the Framers' final answer to this threat. Their goal was not to criminally punish presidents for abuse or corruption; that they left to prosecutors and courts. The Framers had a much greater purpose in mind: the preservation of the Republic itself.

---

[224] *See* Whittington, *Yes, the Senate Can Try Trump.*
[225] *Id.*
[226] *Youngstown Sheet & Tube Co. v. Sawyer*, 343 U.S. 579, 640 (Jackson, J., concurring).
[227] 2 Max Farrand, ed., *The Records of the Federal Convention of 1787*, 67 (1911)

To achieve that purpose, the Framers vested Congress with the power to investigate, impeach, and convict officials for constitutional offenses. The Framers then provided two separate remedies, both focused on an offender's ability to seek and exercise government power: removal from office and disqualification from future officeholding. As confirmed by their deliberations at the Constitutional Convention, as well as the text and structure of the Constitution, the Framers adhered to British and early state practice in authorizing impeachment for *any* high crimes and misdemeanors against the American people—whenever committed and whenever discovered.

That is not surprising. The Framers were too savvy to make up a new rule, at odds with centuries of historical practice, that would allow officials to escape accountability by resigning at the last minute, or by waiting until near the end of their tenure in office to commit abuses, or by concealing misconduct until after they left public service. This would create extremely dangerous and perverse incentives, especially for Presidents who sought to retain power by subverting election results in their final days. In designing the Constitution, the Framers aimed to ensure that the President could never become a King; they did not leave the Nation unprotected against abuse surrounding the transfer of power from one administration to the next.

To that end, the Constitution establishes a clear framework. The House has the sole power to impeach. The Senate has the sole power to try impeachments. These grants of jurisdiction over impeachment are categorical and include no statute of limitations. Any person who commits an extraordinary abuse of power in office may face impeachment for high crimes and misdemeanors. If they are currently a civil officer and are convicted, they must at least be removed from office. And in all events, the Senate's judgment in an impeachment case cannot extend further than disqualification from holding any office of honor, trust, or profit under the United States. These rules arise directly from the history, text, and structure of the Constitution.

1. The Constitutional Convention

The Framers were familiar with the history of impeachment. They understood that the Constitution's references to "impeachment" incorporated centuries of prior practice. In certain very specific respects, they decided to vary from that history—for instance, by requiring a two-thirds supermajority in the Senate to convict. But *nobody* at the Constitutional Convention suggested departing from the existing practice that former officials could be impeached (and disqualified from future officeholding) for their abuses while in office. If anything, the opposite is true. Four aspects of the Framers' deliberations signal their intent to follow historical practice.

First, in debating the standard for impeachable offenses, George Mason explicitly raised the ongoing case of Warren Hastings—and did so to describe when impeachment *should* occur. Were anybody present at the Convention opposed to authorizing the impeachment of former officials, this would have been an obvious opportunity to speak up. "If Mason and the Framers knew anything about the Hastings case," it was that he faced an impeachment proceeding in Parliament *after* he had left his position as Governor General of Bengal.[228] Yet nobody objected. "Given the prominence of the Hastings's impeachment to the framers, the absence of debate on the question at the federal or state ratifying conventions . . . speaks volumes."[229]

Second, and highly relevant here, many Framers described efforts to overturn or corrupt elections as the paradigm case for impeachment. Gouverneur Morris explained that "the Executive ought [] to be impeachable for … Corrupting his electors."[230] William Davie favored impeachment

---

[228] Kalt, *Former Officials*, at 47.

[229] Laurence H. Tribe, *The Senate Can Constitutionally Hold An Impeachment Trial After Trump Leaves Office*, New York Times (Jan. 13, 2021).

[230] 2 Farrand, Records of the Federal Convention, at 69.

for a President who spared "no efforts or means whatever to get himself re-elected."[231] And Mason intended impeachment for a President "who has practiced corruption & by that means procured his appointment in the first instance."[232] By necessity, this kind of misconduct would usually occur near the end of a President's term in office.[233] Given their intense focus on danger to elections and the peaceful transfer of power, it is inconceivable that the Framers designed impeachment to be virtually useless in a President's final days, when opportunities to interfere with the peaceful transfer of power would be most tempting and dangerous. Moreover, it would have made no sense for the Framers to allow impeachment if a President succeeded in winning re-election through corrupt means, but to prohibit *any* Congressional response if his efforts to corrupt the election fell short. A President who tried and narrowly failed to retain power improperly could easily try again. He would still warrant disqualification, both to protect the nation from his future wrongdoing and as a deterrent to anybody else contemplating last-ditch attacks on the electoral process.

Indeed, "a singular concern of the Framers in devising our constitutional system was the danger of a power-seeking populist of the type they referred to as a 'demagogue.'"[234] Madison and Hamilton repeatedly warned against this ancient threat to the young Republic.[235] Yet "the Framers further understood that the source of such a person's power does not expire if he or she is expelled from office; so long as such a person retains the loyalty of his or her supporters, he or she might return to power."[236] Accordingly, "the Framers devised the disqualification power to guard against

---

[231] *Id.* at 64.

[232] *Id.* at 65.

[233] *See* Jed Shugerman, *An Originalist Case for Impeaching Ex-Presidents: Mason, Randolph, and Gouverneur Morris*, Shugerblog (Jan. 16, 2021) ("[T]he Framers supported a broad impeachment process for presidential misconduct at the end of their terms, especially with respect to re-election abuses [and] corrupting or contesting electors . . .").

[234] *Letter from Constitutional Law Scholars on Impeaching Former Officers.*

[235] *See* Jeffrey Rosen, *American is Living James Madison's Nightmare*, The Atlantic (October 2018).

[236] *Letter from Constitutional Law Scholars on Impeaching Former Officers.*

that possibility, and would surely disagree that a person who sought to overthrow our democracy could not be disqualified from holding a future office of the United States because the plot reached its crescendo too close to the end of his or her term."[237]

Third, those who wrote and ratified the Constitution saw that impeachment was meant to deter abuse of office—which it could not achieve if wrongdoers knew they could easily escape any inquiry or trial. At the Convention, Davie described impeachment as "an essential security for the good behaviour of the Executive."[238] In Massachusetts, Reverend Samuel Stillman warned, "With such a prospect [of impeachment], who will dare to abuse the powers vested in him by the people."[239] In North Carolina, future Justice James Iredell stated, "[Impeachment] will be not only the means of punishing misconduct, but it will prevent misconduct."[240] And in Federalist No. 64, future Chief Justice John Jay wrote, "so far as the fear of punishment and disgrace can operate, that motive to good behavior is amply afforded by the article on the subject of impeachments."[241]

If all it took to evade impeachment were quitting—or delaying misconduct until the end of a term—then Davie, Stillman, Iredell, and Jay badly misjudged its deterrent effect. The Framers did not commit such a glaring blunder. To protect the Republic, they designed the impeachment power to cover *anyone* who engaged in abuse or corruption while entrusted with public office—thereby ensuring that any wrongdoer's "infamy might be rendered conspicuous, historic, eternal, in order to prevent the occurrence of likely offenses in the future."[242]

---

[237] *Id.*
[238] 2 Farrand, *Records of the Federal Convention*, at 64.
[239] 2 Jonathan Elliot, ed., *The Debates in the Several State Conventions on the Adoption of the Federal Constitution* 169 (1861)
[240] 4 *id.* at 32.
[241] Federalist 64
[242] *Belknap Proceedings* at 203 (Mr. Manager Knott)

Fourth, and finally, the Framers saw themselves not as restricting the impeachment power in comparison to the states, but rather as broadening it. Federalist No. 39 illustrates the point. There, Madison compared the state and federal governments. Turning to impeachment, he first remarked that "several of the States" did not allow impeachment of "the chief magistrate," adding that "in Delaware and Virginia he is not impeachable till out of office."[243] In contrast, he noted, "the President of the United States is impeachable at any time during his continuance in office."[244] Read in isolation, this may suggest that only a current official can be impeached, but in context it reflects Madison's pride that the President is subject to a *broader* impeachment power than in states that confined impeachment only to former officials. Hamilton confirmed this point in Federalist No. 69. While discussing impeachment, he wrote: "[T]he President of Confederated America would stand upon no better ground than a governor of New York, and upon worse ground than the governors of Maryland and Delaware."[245] Here, too, the upshot is that the President is even *more* accountable than state officials—including in states, like Delaware, that provided for the impeachment of former governors. Neither Hamilton nor Madison suggests any departure from the rule that a former official can be impeached for their abuses in office; instead, they celebrate the extension of the impeachment power to also encompass (and permit the removal of) current officeholders.

All these sources confirm that the Framers intended the impeachment power to reach both current and former officials who engaged in gross abuse of their office. The text and structure of the Constitution that emerged from their debates reflect—in fact, *require*—that conclusion.

---

[243] Federalist No. 39
[244] *Id.*
[245] Federalist No. 69.

2. Constitutional Text and Structure

The Constitution contains several provisions addressing impeachment. A careful review of the Constitution's text and structure permits only a single conclusion: that the Senate has jurisdiction to hear this trial against President Trump for the constitutional offenses that he committed against the American people while he was entrusted with our highest political office.

The Constitution's impeachment provisions are properly understood by reference to the overarching constitutional plan. Senator John H. Mitchell of Oregon thus explained during the Belknap trial that each provision's "particular location in the Constitution" must "receive consideration in giving construction to its purpose."[246] So that is how we will approach them.

Article I of the Constitution defines the powers of the Legislative Branch. Here, the Constitution uses unqualified language to vest the House and Senate with jurisdiction over all impeachments. That grant of authority does not contain any statute of limitations or any other language limiting Congress's impeachment jurisdiction over people who committed high crimes and misdemeanors while in office. Article I also provides for two separate possible judgments in any impeachment case: removal and disqualification. Nowhere does the Constitution suggest that an impeachment is permitted only when both judgments can be imposed. Instead, it treats them as distinct penalties, mandating only that the Senate not exceed them in rendering judgment. The separate availability of disqualification—without any suggestion that it must necessarily follow removal—confirms that former officials like President Trump can be tried by the Senate. Finally, Article I refers to a "Person" and a "Party" (but not a "civil Officer") in describing the accused in an impeachment. This broader word choice plainly encompasses former officials.

---

[246] *Belknap Proceedings* at 347 (Senator Mitchell).

Whereas Article I addresses the Legislative Branch, Article II concerns the Executive Branch. It refers to impeachment only twice—and on both occasions it *restrains* the Executive's power to resist an impeachment: first by confirming that the President's pardon power cannot defeat impeachments; and second by requiring at least the removal of any current officer convicted of an impeachable offense. Neither of these provisions limits the jurisdiction of the Senate over President Trump or makes the possibility of removal a requirement of impeachment.

a. Article I of the Constitution

Article I sets up the Legislative Branch of the federal government. In Section 2, it vests the House with the "sole Power of Impeachment." This is an "express, distinct, positive, absolute and unqualified grant of jurisdictional power to the House of Representatives to impeach."[247] And as explained above, the phrase "Power of Impeachment" had a well-defined, well-developed meaning in the 1780s that the Framers understood to encompass former officers. Whenever the House exercises its "sole Power of Impeachment," the Senate has comprehensive, exclusive jurisdiction under Article I, Section 3, which vests it with "the sole Power to try all Impeachments."

These are the *only* provisions anywhere in the Constitution that affirmatively vest and define the jurisdiction of the House and Senate in matters of impeachment. Both of them provide broad authority, with no statute of limitations, no restriction based on whether a person is still in office, and no other caveats based on *when* the accused committed their high crimes and misdemeanors. By its plain and categorical language, the Constitution vests the Senate with full jurisdiction to hear any valid impeachment case brought by the House for high crimes and misdemeanors. And it makes

---

[247] *Id.* at 338 (Senator Mitchell).

perfectly clear that the Senate is empowered to "try all Impeachments," which at bare minimum must include jurisdiction where the House impeached an official while he was still in office.

As a result, any claim that Congress lacks authority to impeach and convict a former official must arise not from jurisdictional language in the text itself, but from supposed implications of the text. Yet a careful study of the Constitution instead confirms that the Framers intended impeachment to reach anyone who abused power while in office.

This is clear from Article I, Section 3, Clause 7: "Judgment in Cases of Impeachment *shall not extend further* than to removal from Office, and disqualification to hold and enjoy any Office of honor, Trust or Profit under the United States" (emphasis added). In interpreting this language, we must assign meaning to every word. Following that rule, this provision can only be read as "fixing a minimum and maximum penalty."[248] As Professor McConnell explains, "the clause does not say that both sanctions are required; it says that the judgment may not go beyond imposition of both sanctions."[249] Therefore, "the clause does not require removal; it just precludes the Senate from imposing penalties like fines, imprisonment or death."[250] This language limits the possible remedies as compared to British impeachment, "in which the full range of criminal penalties was available." [251]

Under Clause 7, when the Senate convicts, it (1) may remove the accused if they are in office and (2) separately, it may impose disqualification. What it may not do is impose judgments that "extend further" than those options. Critically, "these 'judgments'—removal and disqualification—

---

[248] C.S. Potts, *Impeachment As A Remedy*, 12 St. Louis L. Rev. 15, 23 (1926).

[249] Quoted in Eugene Volokh, *Impeaching Officials While They're in Office, but Trying Them After They Leave*, The Volokh Conspiracy (Jan. 28, 2021), https://reason.com/volokh/2021/01/28/impeaching-officials-while-theyre-in-office-but-trying-them-after-they-leave/

[250] Brian Kalt, *The Constitutional Case for Allowing Late Impeachment Trials*, The Hill (Jan. 29, 2021), https://thehill.com/opinion/judiciary/536487-the-constitutional-case-for-allowing-late-impeachment-trials

[251] *Id.*

are analytically distinct and linguistically divisible."[252] The text does not say "removal from Office, and *then* disqualification" or "removal from Office, *followed by* disqualification." It simply identifies two separate possible sentences and provides that the Senate cannot exceed them. "[T]he inclusion of both present removal and future disqualification as penalties for impeachment suggests that they are two separate penalties that may be separately applied."[253]

In fact, given how the Senate has historically structured its proceedings, it is *impossible* for the Senate to impose disqualification on a current official: it can disqualify only a former official. If the accused is currently in office, and is convicted by the Senate, they are removed upon conviction. By the time Senators separately vote on disqualification, they are considering what penalty to inflict on someone who is at that point a former officer. In this respect, removal and disqualification must be separate penalties—and disqualification must be available for former officials—because disqualification "is itself necessarily a vote about a former (as opposed to current) officer."[254]

Impeachment thus has "two aspects"—and the Constitution "must be read so as to give full effect to both aspects of this power."[255] It provides for removal from office, and it separately provides for disqualification from future officeholding. Consistent with that understanding, "of the eight officers the Senate has ever voted to remove, it subsequently voted to disqualify only three of them—reinforcing that removal and disqualification are separate inquiries."[256]

Ultimately, neither removal nor disqualification is itself the purpose of impeachment. They both serve the deeper purpose of protecting public against officials who have proven themselves a

---

[252] Tribe, *The Senate Can Constitutionally Hold An Impeachment Trial After Trump Leaves Office.*
[253] Michael J. Gerhardt, *The Federal Impeachment Process: A Constitutional and Historical Analysis* 79-80 (1996).
[254] Stephen I. Vladeck, *Why Trump Can Be Convicted Even as an Ex-President*, New York Times (Jan. 14, 2020).
[255] *Letter from Constitutional Law Scholars on Impeaching Former Officers.*
[256] Vladeck, *Why Trump Can Be Convicted Even as an Ex-President.*

threat to our Constitution. And that purpose would be obstructed if Clause 7 were distorted by an interpretation that precluded the impeachment of former officials. This would create incentives for a President "to behave only early in his term, to conceal his wrongdoing long enough to run out the clock, and to skip out of office if congressional action becomes a serious issue."[257] To ensure that the impeachment power promotes integrity in office, the Constitution must be given its natural reading—one that treats the judgment of disqualification as a distinct remedy that can be imposed on both current and former officials following conviction by the Senate.

Although President Trump may argue that Clause 7 limits impeachment only to cases where removal can occur, that view is mistaken. As explained, it clashes with the text of the Constitution. Further, it rests on a logical fallacy. Clause 7 bars the Senate from imposing any sentence *beyond* removal or disqualification. But "a prohibition against doing more than two things cannot be turned into a command to do both or neither."[258] "It certainly will not be seriously maintained that, when a statute prescribes two punishments, one of which has become impossible, the offender is thereby exempted from the other."[259] Such analysis collapses upon scrutiny: in authorizing two possible penalties upon conviction, and saying the Senate may not exceed them, the Constitution did not confer a right on the accused to escape trial entirely because one of the penalties is unavailable. If a defendant made that contention in court, her argument would be rejected out of hand.

That position is especially untenable because it would give abusive officials total control over their own impeachment proceedings. Any official "who betrayed the public trust and was impeached could avoid accountability simply by resigning one minute before the Senate's final

---

[257] Kalt, *Former Officials*, at 71-72.
[258] Belknap Proceedings at 277 (Senator Edmunds).
[259] Id. at 193 (Mr. Manager Hoar).

conviction vote."[260] Needless to say, there is an overwhelming presumption against "a proposition that makes the jurisdiction of the Senate depend upon the will of the accused," and that "would practically annihilate the power of impeachment in all cases of guilt clearly provable."[261] The Framers did not design the Constitution's mightiest safeguards to be so easily undermined. As House Manager James Proctor Knott of Kentucky explained to the Senate during the trial of Secretary Belknap, the ultimate question is simply stated: "Whether you exercise the functions devolved upon you today as the highest court known to our Government by virtue of a constitutional power, or merely at the will and pleasure of the accused."[262]

To ask that question is to answer it. The Framers authorized disqualification for a reason. They knew that in especially grievous cases, a failure to impeach and disqualify could imperil the nation—both by setting a dangerous precedent and by allowing an official to repeat his misconduct. It is implausible that the Framers structured impeachment to allow abusive officials, at their own discretion, to readily escape trial, judgment, and disqualification. Instead, the Framers adhered to established English and state practice. And they used language in Article I, Section 3, Clause 7 that very clearly treats removal and disqualification as separate possible judgments upon conviction. It is therefore wrong to assert that "removal from office is the sole object of impeachment," since "the Constitution authorizes a sentence of disqualification that may be as properly pronounced against the man who has left office as against him who clings to it."[263]

That conclusion is confirmed (and independently required) by the language used in the impeachment provisions of Article I, Section 3, Clauses 6 and 7:

---

260 *Letter from Constitutional Law Scholars on Impeaching Former Officers.*
261 *Id.* at 247 (Senator Thurman).
262 *Id.* at 144 (Mr. Manager Knott).
263 *Id.* at 250 (Senator Thurman).

> The Senate shall have the sole Power to try all Impeachments. When sitting for that Purpose, they shall be on Oath or Affirmation. When the President of the United States is tried, the Chief Justice shall preside: And no **Person** shall be convicted without the Concurrence of two thirds of the Members present.
>
> Judgment in Cases of Impeachment shall not extend further than to removal from Office, and disqualification to hold and enjoy any Office of honor, Trust or Profit under the United States: but the **Party** convicted shall nevertheless be liable and subject to Indictment, Trial, Judgment and Punishment, according to Law.

(emphasis added).

The word choice here is significant, especially in contrast to Article II, Section 4 of the Constitution, which provides that "all civil Officers of the United States" must be removed from office upon conviction for impeachable offenses. Unlike that provision, Article I—which creates the impeachment power and vests Congress with jurisdiction—does not refer to "civil Officers." Instead, in describing who may be subject to impeachment, it uses broader language: "Person" and "Party." The Framers chose their words carefully. They could have written "civil Officers" in Article I to describe who can be impeached, yet they did not do so. It follows that there must be a "Person" or "Party" subject to impeachment who is not a "civil Officer[]." But in order to face impeachment, a person must commit high crimes and misdemeanors, which by definition only a government official can do. That leaves only a single possible explanation for why the Framers used "Person" and "Party" rather than "civil Officers" in Article I, Section 3: they wanted to ensure that the text of the Constitution covered the impeachment, conviction, and disqualification of *former* officials for high crimes and misdemeanors committed while they were in office.[264]

---

[264] *Id.* at 403-404 (Senator Bayard).

b. Article II of the Constitution

Article II defines and limits the authority of the Executive Branch. As a review of its plain text confirms, Article II "contains no grant of power" to any branch of government on the subject of impeachment.[265] Instead, it addresses impeachment only twice and, significantly, only to *constrain* the Executive Branch. Although President Trump may attempt to rely on language in Article II to contest the Senate's jurisdiction over him, any such reliance would be misplaced.

First consider Article II, Section 2, which provides that the President "shall have Power to grant Reprieves and Pardons for Offenses against the United States, *except in Cases of Impeachment*" (emphasis added). This rule reflects a critical feature of the Constitution's design: because impeachment "is a great check upon misconduct in the executive branch . . . the power of impeachment and conviction is placed as far as possible beyond the influence of or interference by the executive branch or any member therefore."[266] An impeachment proceeding is not subject to a Presidential veto. It does not depend upon support from federal prosecutors (who serve in the Executive Branch). It can override the President's ordinarily sweeping discretion to select his own officers. And a President cannot use his pardon power to prevent Congress from impeaching and convicting anyone who has committed a great and dangerous offense. These aspects of impeachment are essential to its role in the separation of powers. The jurisdiction and authority of Congress in matters of impeachment are not subject to control by the Executive Branch; after all, a major purpose of the impeachment power is to restrain the Executive Branch.

---

265 *Id.* at 299-300 (Senator Wright).
266 *Id.* at 402 (Senator Bayard).

This principle confirms that former officials must be subject to impeachment for any and all abuses committed while in office. Under the Appointments Clause—which appears in Article II of the Constitution—the President enjoys a broad "removal power."[267] This allows him to fire many officials within the Executive Branch. If only current officials could be impeached for high crimes and misdemeanors, the President could easily stop impeachments by firing officials accused (or suspected) of high crimes and misdemeanors. That would prevent Congress from getting to the bottom of what happened. It would also weaken the deterrent effect of impeachment, and allow the President to block the Senate from convicting and disqualifying officials who deserve it.

Again, the Framers were not foolish. The Constitution does not enable the President to accomplish through his removal power the very same interference with impeachment that it forbids by expressly limiting his pardon power. As explained above, it allows the impeachment of former officials for abuses committed in office, thus ensuring that the President's power to fire officials cannot halt an impeachment. This rule also avoids another awkward result: if only current officials could be impeached, a President might face a choice between leaving a scofflaw in office (so that an impeachment process could unfold) or immediately firing him to protect the public (which would also stop the impeachment and make it impossible for the Senate to impose disqualification, even if fully warranted).[268] As a matter of constitutional text and structure—not to mention common sense—Article II, Section 2 strongly supports the conclusion that former officials remain subject to impeachment and trial for grievous abuses committed during their tenure in office.

---

[267] *Seila Law LLC v. C.F.P.B.*, 140 S. Ct. 2183, 2197 (2020)
[268] *See* Kalt, *Former Officials*, at 78.

So does Article II, Section 4: "The President, Vice President and all civil Officers of the United States, shall be removed from Office on Impeachment for, and Conviction of, Treason, Bribery, or other high Crimes and Misdemeanors." President Trump may cite this provision to argue that only current officials can be impeached, but that argument has no basis in the text.

Article II, Section 4 states a straightforward rule: whenever a civil officer is impeached and convicted for high crimes and misdemeanors, they "shall be removed." Absolutely nothing about this rule implies, let alone requires, that former officials—who can still face disqualification—are immune from impeachment and conviction. That is unsurprising, since this provision is contained in a part of the Constitution addressed only to current officers, whereas the impeachment provisions set forth in Article I use broader language and emerge from a tradition that covers former officials. Indeed; it would be strange for a provision concerning what happens when a civil officer is convicted to somehow indirectly control the Senate's power under Article I to try all impeachments. As Professor McConnell observes, Article II, Section 4 "does not limit the power of the Senate to try, which comes from Article I, Section 3, Clause 6. It merely states that removal from office is mandatory upon conviction of any sitting officer. No lesser sanction will suffice."[269]

It is therefore a mistake to read Article II, Section 4 as somehow providing protection to officials who abuse their power but escape impeachment while in office (*e.g.*, by committing abuse in their final days, or by concealing wrongdoing, or by resigning at the last minute). Like the rule that pardons cannot defeat an impeachment, the rule set forth in Section 4 is meant to *restrain* the Executive Branch—and it does so by establishing a baseline requirement that officials at least be removed if convicted of impeachable offenses. Thus, whereas the first half of Section 4 concerns

---

[269] Quoted in Volokh, *Impeaching Officials While They're In Office But Trying Them After They Leave.*

itself generally with the requirements for conviction (high crimes and misdemeanors), the second half speaks only about the consequences of convicting a current officer (removal from office).

President Trump may argue that Article II, Section 4 makes removal the primary purpose of *any* impeachment, and that it is strange to imagine an impeachment trial that cannot result in removal. Yet that misreads both Section 4 and Article I. "The fact that the Constitution empowers the Senate to disqualify, as well as remove from office, would, it seems, be a perfect answer to the assumption that the sole purpose of impeachment is the removal from office."[270] The Senate's own practice reflects this: "Senators vote 'guilty' or 'not guilty.' Their formal verdict is not 'remove' or 'don't remove.'"[271] Further, the purpose of impeachment is to protect the nation by deterring official misconduct and ensuring accountability for those who abuse power. Removal and disqualification are each methods of achieving that purpose, which would be hindered rather than furthered if officials knew they could escape any reckoning through resignation or by waiting until their last days in office. "It certainly makes no sense for presidents who commit misconduct late in their terms . . . to be immune from the one process the Constitution allows for barring them from serving in any other federal office or from receiving any federal pensions."[272]

In the alternative, President Trump might contend that the reference to "civil Officers" in Article II means that only government officials—and not private citizens—can ever be subject to impeachment. The flaw in this argument is obvious: "[P]residents and the other officials who are subject to impeachment are not like the rest of us. Once they leave office and return to their private lives, they are still ex-presidents and former officials who may have committed impeachable offenses

---

[270] Id. at 350 (Senator Mitchell).
[271] Brian Kalt, *The Constitutional Case For Allowing Late Impeachment Trials*.
[272] Michael J. Gerhardt, *The Constitution's Option for Impeachment After a President Leaves Office*, Just Security (Jan. 8, 2021).

in office."[273] In other words, impeaching a former official for their official acts while they were a "civil Officer[]" is not the same as impeaching a private citizen. The Constitution "demands of all its officials purity, honesty, and fidelity, and it is plain enough and strong enough to enforce its demands at all times and upon every class of those who enjoy its high places."[274] There is thus no basis for President Trump to object to the Senate's jurisdiction over him (or to raise related Bill of Attainder Clause concerns). The trial of a former official for abuses he committed as an official—arising from an impeachment that also occurred while he was in office—poses no risk of subjecting private parties to punitive legislative action targeting their private conduct.

Next, President Trump may argue that it somehow matters that Chief Justice Roberts is not presiding over this trial. It does not. Under Article I, Section 3, "When the President of the United States is tried, the Chief Justice shall preside." But under Article II, there is only ever a single person at a time who is "the President of the United States." That person is now Joseph R. Biden, Jr. As a former official, President Trump does not trigger the requirement that the Chief Justice preside. Moreover, the reason the Chief Justice is summoned is to ensure the Vice President does not preside over a trial where conviction would result in her becoming the President; obviously, that concern is not implicated in the trial of a *former* president. The normal rules for a Senate trial therefore apply—including those governing who presides (which allow the President *pro tempore* to do so).[275]

---

[273] *Id.*

[274] *Belknap Proceedings* at 255 (Senator Wallace).

[275] President Trump may separately contend that the Constitution does not permit a person to be disqualified from seeking the Presidency. But as the DOJ Office of Legal Counsel concluded under President Obama, "The President surely 'hold[s] an[] Office of Profit or Trust.'" *See* David J. Barron, *Applicability of the Emoluments Clause and the Foreign Gifts and Decorations Act to the President's Receipt of the Nobel Peace Prize*, 33 Op. O.L.C. 1, 4 (2009). Indeed, this is the only conclusion consistent with the text of the Constitution, which repeatedly refers to the President as holding an "Office"—including in the Natural Born Citizen Clause, the Presidential Oath Clause, and the Twelfth, Twenty-Second, and Twenty-Fifth Amendments. *See* Saikrishna Prakash, *Why the Incompatibility Clause Applies to the Office of the President*, 4 Duke J. Const. L. & Pub. Pol'y Sidebar 143 (2009).

Finally, President Trump may assert that finding jurisdiction here will invite the House to undertake a slew of other impeachments, dusting off old issues and pursuing tired grudges. But history disproves such slippery slope concerns. For centuries, the prevailing view—bolstered by the Blount and then Belknap precedents—has been that former officials are subject to impeachment. Yet only in Belknap's case did the House take that step. In the vast majority of cases, including that of President Richard Nixon, the House has properly recognized that an official's resignation or departure abated any need for the extraordinary remedy of impeachment. That remains true today: "There is no likelihood that we shall ever unlimber this clumsy and bulky monster piece of ordinance to take aim at an object from which all danger has gone by."[276] But President Trump's case is exceptional. The danger has not "gone by." The threat to our democracy makes Watergate pale in comparison—and remains with us to this day. Here is the rare case in which love of the Constitution, and commitment to our democracy, required the House to impeach President Trump. And for the same reasons, the Senate can and must take jurisdiction.

C. Congressional Precedent Supports Jurisdiction over President Trump

Prior practice of the House and Senate point the same way as a careful study of the Constitution. Indeed, the case for exercising jurisdiction over President Trump—and convicting him of high crimes and misdemeanors—is even stronger than in any of these precedents.

1. Senator William Blount

The Nation's very first impeachment trial concerned an ex-official: Senator William Blount, who had plotted to give the British control over parts of Florida and Louisiana (which were then

---

[276] *Belknap Proceedings* at 198 (Mr. Manager Hoar).

controlled by Spain and France, respectively).[277] After President Adams provided the House with evidence of this betrayal, the House impeached Blount on July 7, 1797. One day later, by a vote of 25 to 1, the Senate expelled him from its ranks. This was not the end of the matter, however. The House concluded that Blount should also be disqualified from future officeholding, so it proceeded with its investigation and adopted five articles of impeachment on January 29, 1798.[278] Despite Blount's refusal to appear in person, the Senate commenced an impeachment trial with Thomas Jefferson presiding. Ultimately, it dismissed the case on the ground that Members of Congress are not subject to the impeachment power at all. But notably, Blount had also asserted that the Senate lacked jurisdiction over him as a former official—and the Senate did not dismiss on that basis.[279]

2. Secretary of War William Belknap

Nearly eighty years later, in 1876, the House Committee on Expenditures discovered that Secretary of War William Belknap was involved in an elaborate kickback scheme.[280] Hours before the committee released its report, Belknap "rushed to the White House in an unholy panic to tender his resignation," which President Ulysses Grant accepted on the spot.[281] Two hours later, fully aware that Belknap had resigned, the House voted unanimously to impeach him.[282]

The ensuing Senate trial is "the single most important precedent" on the question whether a former official is subject to impeachment.[283] Belknap strenuously argued that the Senate lacked jurisdiction because he had resigned before the House impeached him. The Senate heard "[m]ore

---

277 *See* Bowman & Kalt, *Congress Can Impeach Trump Now And Convict Him When He's Gone.*
278 Eleanore Bushnell, *Crimes, Follies, and Misfortunes: The Federal Impeachment Trials* 30 (1992).
279 *See id.* at 32-41.
280 *See* Kalt, *Former Officials*, at 94.
281 Ron Chernow, *Grant* 821 (2017).
282 Kalt, *Former Officials*, at 95.
283 *Id.* at 94.

than two weeks of wide-ranging arguments on the question . . . followed by two weeks of [S]enators' reciting their own conclusions."[284] After this exhaustive presentation—which covered virtually all of the points likely to be raised here—the Senate voted 37 to 29 that it had jurisdiction over the case. It proceeded to a full presentation of argument and evidence over a two-month period and ultimately acquitted Belknap, though only after plenary consideration of the merits of the case.

3. Judges Robert Archbald & George English

Two cases from the early 1900s further support the Senate's jurisdiction here. The first involved Circuit Judge Robert Archbald, who was impeached in 1912. Of the thirteen articles of impeachment that the House approved, six addressed conduct in his former role as a district judge. In the end, Judge Archbald was convicted on five articles relating to his tenure as a circuit judge; on that basis, he was removed from office and disqualified from future officeholding. The Senate acquitted him of two articles relating to his circuit judgeship, as well as the articles concerning his conduct as a district judge. It is clear from the public record, however, that the case against Judge Archbald relating to his earlier role failed on the merits—and that "a majority of the [S]enators voting saw no problem" with impeaching Judge Archbald for conduct in his former office.[285] Once again, the arguments for jurisdiction over former officials commanded a clear majority in the Senate.

Fourteen years later, the House impeached District Judge George English for corrupt conduct on the bench. Six days before his Senate trial, Judge English resigned. In light of that decision—and given his advanced age—the House resolved that it did "not desire further to urge the articles of impeachment."[286] In a filing with the Senate, however, the House Managers pointedly

---

[284] *Id.* at 96.
[285] *Id.* at 103.
[286] Quoted in *id.* at 104.

stated that "the resignation of Judge English in no way affects the right of the Senate, sitting as a court of impeachment, to hear and determine [the case]."[287] Further, "No [S]enator suggested that it would have been impossible or unconstitutional to proceed if the House had not 'desired' to do otherwise."[288] To the contrary, several Senators stated that the Senate in fact retained jurisdiction. Senator William C. Bruce of Maryland remarked, "I deeply regret the conclusion that the House of Representatives has reached."[289] And Senator Duncan Fletcher of Florida wanted it "distinctly understood" that the case was not precedent for the idea that resignation terminates a trial.[290] Thus, the proceeding against Judge English supports the Senate's jurisdiction over former officials, since "the House and the Senate felt that they could have proceeded with [that] case."[291]

In fact, as noted above, the case for jurisdiction here is stronger than in *any* of the precedents just mentioned. Unlike Senator Blount, who was held accountable through expulsion, President Trump will escape responsibility for his betrayal of the Constitution unless this body tries and convicts him. Unlike Secretary Belknap, who resigned before the House could act, President Trump was impeached by the House while he was still in office. Moreover, whereas Secretary Belknap and Judge English left office in disgrace, President Trump insists that his constitutional offenses were perfectly acceptable—and so the precedent set by a failure to try him would pose an astronomically greater threat to the Republic. Finally, unlike in the case of Judge Archbold, the evidence against President Trump is overwhelming. His is personally responsible for an attack that unleashed death and mayhem at the Capitol amid the transfer of power. For Congress to stand aside in the face of

---

[287] Quoted in *id.*
[288] *Id.* at 105.
[289] Quoted in *id.*
[290] Quoted in *id.*
[291] *Id.* at 106.

such conduct would be a grave abdication of its constitutional duty, and an invitation for future Presidents to act without fear of constraint during their final months in office.

* * * * *

Constitutional history, text, and structure, as well as prior Congressional practice, all confirm that the Senate has jurisdiction to try President Trump. So does common sense. While sworn to faithfully execute the laws—and to preserve, protect, and defend the Constitution—President Trump incited insurrection against the United States government. His conduct endangered the life of every single Member of Congress, jeopardized the peaceful transition of power and line of succession, and compromised our national security. This is *precisely* the sort of constitutional offense that warrants disqualification from federal office. President Trump has proven his willingness to break and brutalize the law in his quest for power. The Senate must establish beyond doubt, for all time, and for officials of all political parties that President Trump's behavior was intolerable.

CONCLUSION

President Trump falsely asserted that he won the 2020 election and then sought to overturn its results. He and his supporters filed dozens of lawsuits nationwide—including before judges he had appointed—but their claims uniformly failed to persuade. He also tried to convince state and federal election officials and law enforcement personnel to attempt to reverse the election outcome. These attempts failed, too. The only honorable path at that point was for President Trump to accept the results and concede his electoral defeat. Instead, he summoned a mob to Washington, exhorted them into a frenzy, and aimed them like a loaded cannon down Pennsylvania Avenue. As the Capitol was overrun, President Trump was reportedly "delighted." And rather than take immediate steps to quell the violence and protect lives, President Trump left his Vice President and Congress to fend for themselves while he lobbied allies to continue challenging election results.

As will be shown at trial, President Trump endangered our Republic and inflicted deep and lasting wounds on our Nation. His conduct resulted in more than five deaths and many more injuries. The Capitol was defiled. The line of succession was imperiled. America's global reputation was damaged. For the first time in history, the transfer of presidential power was interrupted. And the threat of violence remains with us: as President Biden was inaugurated and even now, the Capitol more closely resembles an armed camp than the seat of American democracy.

President Trump's incitement of insurrection requires his conviction and disqualification from future federal officeholding. This is not a case where elections alone are a sufficient safeguard against future abuse; it is the electoral process itself that President Trump attacked and that must be protected from him and anyone else who would seek to mimic his behavior. Indeed, it is difficult to imagine a case that more clearly evokes the reasons why the Framers wrote a disqualification power into the Constitution. The need for conviction and disqualification is further supported by Section 3 of the Fourteenth Amendment, which bars from government service those who "having previously taken an oath … to support the Constitution of the United States, shall have engaged in insurrection or rebellion against the same, or given aid or comfort to the enemies thereof."[292] President Trump's conduct offends everything that the Constitution stands for. The Senate must make clear to him and all who follow that a President who provokes armed violence against the government of the United States in an effort to overturn the results of an election will face trial and judgment.

Many have suggested that we should turn the page on the tragic events of January 6, 2021. But to heal the wounds he inflicted on the Nation, we must hold President Trump accountable for his conduct and, in so doing, reaffirm our core principles. Failure to convict would embolden future

---

[292] U.S. Const. Amend. XIV § 3.

leaders to attempt to retain power by any and all means—and would suggest that there is no line a President cannot cross. The Senate should make clear to the American people that it stands ready to protect them against a President who provokes violence to subvert our democracy.[258]

Respectfully submitted,

Jamie Raskin
Diana DeGette
David Cicilline
Joaquin Castro
Eric Swalwell
Ted Lieu
Stacey Plaskett
Madeleine Dean
Joe Neguse

February 2, 2021

U.S. House of Representatives Managers

[258] The House Managers wish to recognize the invaluable assistance of the following individuals in preparing this trial memorandum: Barry H. Berke, Joshua Matz, and Sarah Istel of the House Committee on the Judiciary; Susanne Sachsman Grooms, Krista Boyd, Candyce Phoenix, Cassie Fields, and Jacob Glick of the House Committee on Oversight and Reform; and Douglas Letter, Megan Barbero, Eric Columbus, Will Havemann, Lisa Helvin, and Jonathan Schwartz of the House Office of General Counsel.

This page intentionally left blank.

IN PROCEEDINGS BEFORE
THE UNITED STATES SENATE

In re:

IMPEACHMENT OF
FORMER PRESIDENT
DONALD J. TRUMP

TRIAL MEMORANDUM
OF DONALD J. TRUMP, 45TH PRESIDENT OF THE UNITED STATES OF AMERICA

Bruce L. Castor, Jr., Esquire
David Schoen, Esquire
Michael T. van der Veen, Esquire
Counsel to the 45th President of the United States

February 8, 2021

TABLE OF CONTENTS

I. INTRODUCTION

During the past four years, Democrat members of the United States House of Representatives have filed at least nine (9) resolutions to impeach Donald J. Trump, the 45th President of the United States,[1] each containing charges more outlandish than the next.[2] One might have been excused for thinking that the Democrats' fevered hatred for Citizen Trump and their "Trump Derangement Syndrome" would have broken by now, seeing as *he is no longer the President*, and yet for the second time in just over a year the United States Senate is preparing to sit as a Court of Impeachment, but this time over a private citizen who is a former President.[3] In this Country, the Constitution – not a political party and not politicians – reigns supreme. But through this latest Article of Impeachment now before the Senate, Democrat politicians seek to carve out a mechanism by which they can silence a political opponent and a minority party. The Senate must summarily reject this brazen political act

This rushed, single article of impeachment ignores the very Constitution from which its power comes and is itself defectively drafted.. In bringing this impeachment at all, the Members of the House leadership have debased the grave power of impeachment and disdained the solemn

---

1 Andrew Kaczynski, Christopher Massie, *A running list of Democrats who have discussed impeachment*, CNN (Mar. 12, 2017), https://www.cnn.com/2017/05/12/politics/kfile-democrats-impeach-trump/index.html

2 Some of the allegations that they thought were grounds for impeachment: national security decisions that were upheld by the Supreme Court, *see Trump v. Hawaii*, 138 S. Ct. 2392 (2018); publishing disparaging tweets about Democratic House members in response to their own attacks on the President, H.R. Res. 498, 116th Cong. (2019); and failing to nominate persons to fill vacancies and insulting the press, H.R. Res. 396, 116th Cong. (2019).

3 The charge itself is not even original: One of the articles of impeachment introduced by Representative Al Green back in December 2017 accused President Trump of "inciting hate and hostility" by "sowing discord among the people of the United States." *Impeaching Donald John Trump, President of the United States, of High Misdemeanors*, H.R. 646, 115th Cong. § 1 (2017).

responsibility that this awesome power entails. In bringing this impeachment in the manner in which they did, namely *via* a process that violated every precedent and every principle of fairness followed in impeachment inquiries for more than 150 years, they offered the public a master's class in the art of political opportunism.

The intellectual dishonesty and factual vacuity put forth by the House Managers in their trial memorandum only serve to further punctuate the point that this impeachment proceeding was never about seeking justice.[4] Instead, this was only ever a selfish attempt by Democratic leadership in the House to prey upon the feelings of horror and confusion that fell upon *all* Americans across the entire political spectrum upon seeing the destruction at the Capitol on January 6 by a few hundred people. Instead of acting to heal the nation, or at the very least focusing on prosecuting the lawbreakers who stormed the Capitol, the Speaker of the House and her allies have tried to callously harness the chaos of the moment for their own political gain.

II. STATEMENT OF FACTS RELEVANT TO THE ARTICLE OF IMPEACHMENT

On January 6, 2021, rioters entered the Capitol building and wrought unprecedented havoc, mayhem, and death. In a brazen attempt to further glorify violence, the House Managers took several pages of their Memorandum to restate over 50 sensationalized media reports detailing the horrific incidents and shocking violence of those hours. Counsel for the 45th President hereby stipulate that what happened at the Capitol by those criminals was horrible and horrific in every sense of those words. Their actions were utterly inexcusable and deserve robust and swift investigation and prosecution. As President Trump said in a video statement of condemnation, "I want to be very clear, I unequivocally condemn the violence that we saw last week. Violence and

---

[4] Hugh Hewitt, *A fast-track impeachment would not be justice*, Washington Post (Jun. 8, 2021), https://www.washingtonpost.com/opinions/2021/01/08/fast-track-trump-impeachment-pointless-revenge/

vandalism have absolutely no place in our country and no place in our movement."[5] Mr. Trump's comments echoed his sentiments expressed the day of the rally, as he repeatedly urged protesters to stay peaceful,[6] and told rioters to go home.[7] [8]

The House Managers' compulsion to obfuscate the truth is borne out of an absence of evidence relied upon in their "Statement of Facts." As the body vested with the sole power to impeach, the House serves as the investigator and prosecutor. There was no investigation. The House abdicated that responsibility to the media. Of the 170 footnotes in the House Manager's Trial Memorandum, there were only three citations to affidavits of four law enforcement officers and they were merely referenced to support descriptions of what rioters were wearing and weapons that were found. The rest of the purported "facts" relied upon by these Constitutionally-charged prosecutors came from hearsay through the media.

---

[5] Reuters, *Trump condemns Capitol Hill violence*, Reuters (Jan. 13, 2021).https://www.reuters.com/article/us-usa-trump-remarks/trump-condemns-capitol-hill-violence-in-video-that-does-not-mention-impeachment-idUSKBN29I37G

[6] Rev.com, *Donald Trump Speech "Save America" Rally Transcript January 6*, Jan. 6, 2021, beginning at approximately 18:16 (emphasis added), available at https://www.rev.com/blog/transcripts/donald-trump-speech-save-america-rally-transcript-january-6. ("Transcript of January 6, 2021 Speech").

[7] Kevin Breuninger, *Trump tells Capitol rioters to 'go home' but repeatedly pushes false claim that election was stolen,* CNBC (Jan. 6, 2021), https://www.cnbc.com/2021/01/06/trump-tells-capitol-rioters-to-go-home-now-but-still-calls-the-election-stolen.html

[8] The House Managers' suggestion that President Trump did not act swiftly enough to quell the violence is absolutely not true. Upon hearing of the reports of violence, he tweeted, pleading with the crowd to be "peaceful," followed by a tweeted video urging people to "go home" and to do so in "peace." He and the White House further took immediate steps to coordinate with authorities to provide whatever was necessary to counteract the rioters. The fact is there are complex procedural elements involved in quelling a riot at the Capitol and on the mall – DC police, Capitol Police, National Guard, etc., There was a flurry of activity inside the White House working to mobilize assets. There is no legitimate proof, nor can there ever be, that President Trump was "delighted" by the events at the Capitol. He, like the rest of the Country, was horrified at the violence.

A. The Single Article Of Impeachment Is Belied By An Analysis Of Mr. Trump's Spoken Words To A Crowd Gathered At The Ellipse Four On January 6, 2021.

At the demand of the Speaker of the House, certain members of the House drafted and introduced Resolution 24 impeaching Mr. Trump, in his capacity as President of the United States. The single Article titled "Incitement of Insurrection" charged Mr. Trump with engaging in "high Crimes and Misdemeanors by inciting violence against the Government of the United States." Incitement is the act of encouraging someone to do or feel something unpleasant or violent.[9] An insurrection – unlike a riot – is an organized movement acting for the express purpose to overthrow and take possession of a government's powers.[10] President's Trump speech on January 6, 2021 was not an act encouraging an organized movement to overthrow the Unites States government.

On January 6, 2021, Mr. Trump addressed a crowd of people who had gathered on the Ellipse, public land that is part of the President's Park next to the White House. Mr. Trump spoke for approximately one hour and fifteen minutes. Of the over 10,000 words spoken, Mr. Trump used the word "fight" a little more than a handful of times and each time in the figurative sense that has long been accepted in public discourse when urging people to stand and use their voices to be heard on matters important to them; it was not and could not be construed to encourage acts of violence Notably absent from his speech was any reference to or encouragement of an insurrection, a riot, criminal action, or any acts of physical violence whatsoever. The only reference to force was in taking pride in his administration's creation of the Space Force. Mr. Trump never made any express or implied mention of weapons, the need for weapons, or anything

---

9 https://dictionary.cambridge.org/us/dictionary/english/incitement

10 Younis Bros. & Co. v. Cigna Worldwide Ins. Co., 899 F. Supp. 1385, 1392-1393 (E.D. Pa. 1995) (*citing Pan American World Airways, Inc. v. Aetna Casualty & Surety Co.*, 505 F.2d 989, 1017 (2d Cir. 1974) *Holiday Inns, Inc. v. Aetna Ins. Co.*, 571 F. Supp. 1460, 1487 (S.D.N.Y. 1983); and *Home Ins. Co. of New York v. Davila*, 212 F.2d 731, 736 (1st Cir.1954)).

of the sort. Instead, he simply called on those gathered to ***peacefully and patriotically use their voices***.

Mr. Trump greeting the crowd by remarking on the honor he felt looking out at the many "American patriots who are committed to the honesty of our elections and integrity of our glorious Republic." He went on to thank the crowd for their "extraordinary love" noting "that's what it is. There's never been a movement like this ever, ever for the extraordinary love for this amazing country and this amazing movement. Thank you." Mr. Trump told those gathered that "we're gathering in the heart of our Nation's Capital for one very, very basic and simple reason, to save our democracy."

Nearly twenty minutes into his speech, Mr. Trump said "I know that everyone here will soon be marching over to the Capitol building to ***peacefully and patriotically*** make your voices heard." Mr. Trump then spent approximately thirty to forty (30 – 40) minutes recapping some of his accomplishments as President and his beliefs on the outcome of the election, including the voting irregularities he attributed to the changes made in various states purportedly in response to the pandemic, and his conversation with Georgia's secretary of state.

As Mr. Trump was winding down his speech, he again looked out at all those gathered saying "looking out at all the amazing patriots here today, I have never been more confident in our nation's future." Although expressing some caution, Mr. Trump added "we are the greatest country on earth and we are headed, were headed, in the right direction." With great hope, Mr. Trump went on to state:

> As this enormous crowd shows, we have truth and justice on our side. We have a deep and enduring love for America in our hearts. We love our country. We have overwhelming pride in this great country, and we have it deep in our souls. Together we are determined to defend and preserve government of the people, by the people and for the people.

> Our brightest days are before us, our greatest achievements still wait. I think one of our great achievements will be election security because nobody until I came along, had any idea how corrupt our elections were. And again, most people would stand there at 9:00 in the evening and say, "I want to thank you very much," and they go off to some other life, but I said, "Something's wrong here. Something's really wrong. Can't have happened." And we fight. We fight like Hell and if you don't fight like Hell, you're not going to have a country anymore.
>
> Our exciting adventures and boldest endeavors have not yet begun. My fellow Americans for our movement, for our children and for our beloved country and I say this, despite all that's happened, the best is yet to come.

Mr. Trump concluded his speech at the Ellipse stating "[s]o let's walk down Pennsylvania Avenue. I want to thank you all. God bless you and God Bless America. Thank you all for being here, this is incredible. Thank you very much. Thank you." Despite the House Managers' charges against Mr. Trump, his statements cannot and could not reasonably be interpreted as a call to immediate violence or a call for a violent overthrown of the United States' government.

B. Democrat Members Of The House Drafted The Article Of Impeachment Before Any Investigation Into The Riot Had Even Started.

Democrat members of the House Judiciary Committee publically admitted that they began drafting the Article of Impeachment moments after angry extremists breached the doors of the Capitol.[11] The very next day, Speaker Nancy Pelosi and Senate Democratic Leader Chuck Schumer called on Vice-President Pence to invoke the 25th Amendment concluding – without any investigation – that Mr. Trump incited the insurrection and continued to pose an imminent danger

---

[11] Jennifer Haberkorn, *Sheltering in a Capitol Office: a California Lawmaker's Frantic Text Got the Impeachment Ball Rolling,* L.A. Times (Jan. 13, 2021), https://www.latimes.com/politics/story/2021-01-13/sheltering-in-a-capitol-office-a-california-lawmakers-frantic-text-got-the-impeachment-ball-rolling

if he remained in office as President.[12] Five days later, on January 11, 2020, House Democrats formally introduced House Resolution 24. On January 12th, Speaker Pelosi announced the nine representatives who would serve as the impeachment managers. One day later, on January 13th, House Democrats completed the fastest presidential impeachment inquiry in history and adopted the Article of Impeachment over strong opposition and with zero due process afforded to Mr. Trump, against Constitutional requirements and centuries of practice.[13]

C. The House Managers' "Statement Of Facts" Outlines A Narrative Irrelevant To The Facts Alleged In Support Of The Single Article Of Impeachment.

The House Managers spent nearly thirty-five (35) of their seventy-seven (77) page Trial Memorandum rehashing stories written by the media of mischaracterized statements attributed to Mr. Trump many months *before* Mr. Trump addressed the crowd at the Ellipse in Washington, D.C. on January 6, 2021. Media reports and reporters' opinions are not facts and most assuredly are not facts that should form the basis for instituting the grave power of impeachment. More significantly, however, Mr. Trump was never charged in the Article of Impeachment with the claims made in these various reports.

1. Law Enforcement Had Reports Of A Potential Attack On The Capitol Several Days Before President Trump's Speech.

Despite going to great lengths to include irrelevant information regarding Mr. Trump's comments dating back to August 2020 and various postings on social media, the House Managers are silent on one very chilling fact. The Federal Bureau of Investigation has confirmed that the

---

12 *Pelosi, Schumer Joint Statement on Call to Vice President Pence on Invoking 25th Amendment*, (Jan. 7, 2021), https://www.speaker.gov/newsroom/1721-0

13 H.Res.24 – Impeaching Donald John Trump, President of the United States, for high crimes and misdemeanors, 117th Congress (2021-2022), https://www.congress.gov/bill/117th-congress/house-resolution/24/actions

breach at the Capitol was planned *several days* in advance of the rally, and therefore had nothing to do with the President's speech on January 6th at the Ellipse. According to investigative reports all released after January 6, 2021, "the Capitol Police, the NYPD and the FBI all had prior warning there was going to be an attack on the Capitol..."[14] Embarrassingly enough, even members of the Democratic leadership themselves have admitted on the record, albeit subsequent to January 6, 2021, that they believed the riots were pre-planned, with some, including Representative James C. Clyburn, the House Democratic Whip, going so far as to accuse fellow House Members of coordinating and planning the attack in advance as co-conspirators.[15] The problem with that claim of course is that while the House Managers are clearly eager to make the most of this tragedy for their own purely personal political gain, House Leadership simply cannot have it both ways. Either the *President* incited the riots, like the Article claims, or the riots were pre-planned by a small group of criminals who deserve punishment to the fullest extent of the law. 33 Representatives are only now calling for investigations into Members across the aisle.[16]

---

[14] Ian Schwartz, *John Solomon: Capitol Riot Was A "planned Attack," Can't Blame Trump; What Did Pelosi and McConnell Know?*, Real Clear Politics (Jan. 13, 2021), https://www.realclearpolitics.com/video/2021/01/13/john_solomon_capitol_riot_was_a_planned_attack_cant_blame_trump_what_did_pelosi_mcconnell_know.html

[15] Geoff Earle, *Republican congressman's top aid admits to being with mob*, Daily Mail (Jan. 14, 2021),https://www.dailymail.co.uk/news/article-9147863/Democratic-whip-Jim-Clyburn-says-Democrats-convinced-MAGA-rioters-inside-help.html

[16] Siladitya Ray, *Lawmakers Led "Reconnaissance' Tours of the Capitol,* Forbes (Jan. 13, 2021), https://www.forbes.com/sites/siladityaray/2021/01/13/lawmakers-led-reconnaissance-tours-of-the-capitol-ahead-of-last-weeks-riots-democratic-congresswoman-alleges/?sh=32ec8fe81c7e

The real truth is that the people who criminally breached the Capitol did so of their own accord[17] and for their own reasons, and they are being criminally prosecuted.[18] While never willing to allow a "good crisis" to go to waste, the Democratic leadership is incapable of understanding that not *everything* can always be blamed on their political adversaries, no matter how very badly they may wish to exploit any moment of uncertainty on the part of the American people.[19] Even a cursory investigation would have disproved the House's theory of incitement; however, Speaker Pelosi did not grant the President any of his Constitutionally mandated due process rights.

A simple timeline of events demonstrates conclusively that the riots were not inspired by the President's speech at the Ellipse. "The Capitol is 1.6 miles away from Ellipse Park which is near the White House. This is approximately a 30-33 minute walk. Trump began addressing the crowd at 11:58 AM and made his final remarks at 1:12 PM… Protesters, activists and rioters had

---

[17] Some anti-Trump, some ani-government. *See, e.g.*, Alicia Powe, *Exclusive: "Boogaloo Boi" Leader Who Aligns with Black Lives Matter*, Gateway Pundit, (Jan. 17, 2021), https://www.thegatewaypundit.com/2021/01/boogaloo-boi-leader-aligns-black-lives-matter-boasted-organizing-armed-insurrection-us-capitol/. "The goal of swarming the home of the U.S. House of Representatives and Senate is **"to revel in the breach of security while mocking the defenses that protect tyrants…whether that be Trump or others."** *See also* Robert Mackey, *John Sullivan, Who Filmed Shooting of Ashli Babbitt*, The Intercept (Jan. 14, 2021), https://theintercept.com/2021/01/14/capitol-riot-john-sullivan-ashli-babbitt/ ("The rapper, who later retweeted a brief video clip of himself and Sullivan inside the Rotunda that was broadcast live on CNN, told me in an Instagram message … "I'm far from a Trump supporter…I really don't even get into politics at all. It was an experience for me and that's really the only reason I was there.")

[18] *See, e.g.*, Tom Jackman, Marissa J. Lank, Jon Swaine, *Man who shot video of fatal Capitol shooting is arrested, remains focus of political storm,* Washington Post (Jan. 16, 2021), https://www.washingtonpost.com/nation/2021/01/16/sullivan-video-arrested/.

[19] Over the last four years Donald J. Trump has been blamed for every manner of evil thing, and every crisis or news cycle that left people unsure of what to do was another opportunity to point a finger at the President. For one example, when a celebrity claimed that he was the victim of a violent hate crime, Donald Trump was blamed; and when it turned out that the claim was fraudulent the then-Mayor of Chicago quickly pivoted and *still* blamed President Trump for creating a 'toxic environment.' Howie Carr, *Trump is blamed for everything*, Boston Herald (Mar. 30, 2019), https://www.bostonherald.com/2019/03/30/fault-line-trump-is-blamed-for-everything/.

already breached Capitol Grounds a mile away 19 minutes prior to the end of President Trump's speech."[20]

2. The House Managers False Narrative Rests Entirely On Biased And Mischaracterized Reports By The Media And Cherry-Picked, Non-Contextual Parsing Of Mr. Trump's January 6 Speech.

Contrary to the false narrative set forth by the House Managers, Mr. Trump's speech was never directed to inciting or producing any imminent lawless action. It is important to read the speech in its entirety, because the House Managers played shamefully fast and loose with the truth as they cherry-picked its content along with content from other speeches made to other audiences for their Trial Memorandum, desperately searching for incitement and desperate to deflect attention away from the glaring inability to show an insurrection. And this is no small matter, because their demonstrably false claims go right to the heart of their main allegation.

Democrats cannot pretend that they were confused by the word 'fight' in the context President Trump used it in his speech; Speaker Pelosi has used this word multiple times herself in the context of election security,[21] and the well-known nonprofit started by rising Democratic darling Stacey Abrams and endorsed by none other than Speaker Pelosi[22] is literally called 'Fair Fight,' and it asks people to join the "fight for free and fair elections." And yet in her comments during the impeachment debate Speaker Pelosi adjusted the truth by conflating the parts of the

---

[20] Tayler Hansen, *Independent Journalist Tayler Hansen: A Riot that Turned Deadly, What I Witnessed*, Gateway Pundit (Jan. 28, 2021), https://www.thegatewaypundit.com/2021/01/exclusive-independent-journalist-tayler-hansen-riot-turned-deadly-witnessed-us-capitol-riot/

[21] Press Release, *Pelosi Remarks at Election Security Week of Action Press Conference*, Speaker.gov (Jul. 9, 2019), https://www.speaker.gov/newsroom/7819-2.

[22] Press Release, *Pelosi, Schumer Announce Stacey Abrams To Deliver Democratic Response to President Trump's State of the Union*, Speaker.gov (Jan. 29, 2019), https://www.speaker.gov/newsroom/12919-3.

President's speech in which he talked about marching peacefully to the Capitol and the part of the speech addressing the need to fight for election security. She lied to the American people saying: "They were sent here, sent here by the president, with words such as a cry to fight like hell." Incredibly enough, her very next words were "Words matter. Truth matters. Accountability matters."

Words do matter and the words of President Trump's January 6th speech speak for themselves. President Trump did not direct anyone to commit lawless actions, and the claim that he could be responsible if a small group of criminals (who had come to the capital of their own accord armed and ready for a fight) completely misunderstood him, were so enamored with him and inspired by his words that they *left his speech early*, and then walked a mile and a half away to "imminently" do the opposite of what he had just asked for, is simply absurd. The attack on the Capitol was horrific. Period. But as constitutional professors[23] and experienced practitioners[24] agree, "The president didn't mention violence on Wednesday, much less provoke or incite it.[25] The fact that the House Managers found sheer deceptiveness necessary in the exercise of selectively parsing the words of the former President and quoting him out of context underscores the utter weakness of the House Managers' factual and legal claims. This tact is reminiscent of

---

[23] Such as Andrew Koppelman, a Constitutional Law professor from Northwestern University, who explained "It seems to me the Brandenburg standard requires intention," and noted "It's like the word fight. It's often used as a metaphor. 'Senator X is a fighter. He will fight for you." Mark Sherman, Zeke Miller, *Can Trump be charged with inciting a riot? Legal bar is high*, Associated Press (Jan. 8, 2021), https://apnews.com/article/can-donald-trump-be-charged-incite-riot-3f27e4393e83d2967cf25bd18db5b268

[24] Like Jefrey Scott Shapiro, a former District of Columbia assistant attorney general who has experience successfully – and unsuccessfully – convicting protesters for incitement. Jeffrey Scott Shapiro, *No, Trump Isn't Guilty of Incitement*, Wall Street Journal (Jan. 10, 2021), https://www.wsj.com/articles/no-trump-isnt-guilty-of-incitement-11610303966

[25] *Id.*

Congressman Schiff's manufacturing of a fake conversation between President Trump and Ukrainian President Zelensky.[26]

Truth also matters very much. But Speaker Pelosi and her allies perverted the truth. The day after the riot, sensing a political opportunity, House Leadership decided to forego focusing on the business of the nation and unifying a bitterly divided country to once again endeavor to score political points against Mr. Trump. First, in an attempt to usurp Constitutional power that is not in any way hers, the Speaker demanded that Vice-President Michael Pence or the White House Cabinet invoke the 25th Amendment, threatening to launch an impeachment proceeding if they refused. Four days later, on January 11, 2021, an Article of Impeachment was introduced, which charged President Trump with "incitement of insurrection" against the United States government and "lawless action at the Capitol." See H. Res. 24 (117th Congress (2021-2022). The Speaker made good on her extortionate threat.

Accountability does matter, according to the House Managers, unless you are a Democrat. While fixating on words and sentences taken out of context, the House Managers ignore the many reckless statements made by their Democrat colleagues in the House and Senate. Merely by way of example, one need only search media reports to be reminded of Speaker Pelosi's 2018 hopeful comment when disagreeing with a policy: "I just don't even know why there aren't uprisings all over the country. Maybe there will be."[27] And just last summer, when sustained violent riots were

---

[26] Morgan Chalfant, Trump demands Schiff resign, The Hill (Sept. 17, 2019), https://thehill.com/homenews/administration/463344-trump-demands-schiff-resign.

[27] Douglas Ernst, *Nancy Pelosi wonders why there 'aren't uprisings' across nation: 'Maybe there will be,'* Washington Times (Jan. 14, 2018), https://www.washingtontimes.com/news/2018/jun/14/nancy-pelosi-wonders-why-there-arent-uprisings-acr/

decimating our cities and local businesses, Representative Ayana Pressley went on national TV and said that "there needs to be unrest in the streets."[28]

They also ignore the sheer hypocrisy of their House leader's 4-plus year quest to remove President Trump from office. After the Article was introduced, Speaker Pelosi again gave Vice-President Pence an ultimatum: either he invokes the 25th Amendment within twenty-four hours or the impeachment proceedings would proceed. Vice-President Pence responded in a letter to Speaker Pelosi the following day stating that he would not allow her to usurp constitutional authority that is not hers and extort him (and by extension the Nation) to invoke the 25th Amendment because he believed to do so would not "be in the best interest of our Nation or consistent with our Constitution."[29] Vice-President Pence also noted that Speaker Pelosi was being hypocritical, as she had previously stated that in utilizing the 25th Amendment, "we must be '[v]ery respectful of not making a judgment on the basis of a comment or behavior that we don't like, but [rather must base such a decision] on a medical decision."[30]

III. ARGUMENT

A. The Senate Lacks The Constitutional Jurisdiction To Conduct An Impeachment Trial Of A Former President.

The Constitution of the United States bifurcates the power of impeachment and addresses the issue in four places:

Article I, Section 2, Clause 5:

---

[28] Am Joy, *Post office cuts are wa against American people Pressley says*, MSNBC (Aug. 15, 2020), https://www.msnbc.com/am-joy/watch/post-office-cuts-are-war-against-american-people-pressley-says-90125893871

[29] See Mike Pence's Letter to Nancy Pelosi https://www.cnn.com/2021/01/12/politics/pence-letter/index.html.

[30] *Id.*

> The House of Representatives shall choose their Speaker and other Officers; and shall have the sole Power of Impeachment;[31]
>
> Article I, Section 3, Clauses 6 and 7:
> The Senate shall have the sole Power to try all Impeachments. When sitting for that Purpose, they shall be on Oath or Affirmation. When the President of the United States is tried, the Chief Justice shall preside: And no Person shall be convicted without the Concurrence of two-thirds of the Members present. Judgment in Cases of Impeachment shall not extend further than to removal from Office, and disqualification to hold and enjoy any Office of honor, Trust or Profit under the United States; but the Party convicted shall nevertheless be liable and subject to Indictment, Trial, Judgment and Punishment, according to Law;[32]
>
> Article II, Section 2:
> [The President] ... shall have power to grant reprieves and pardons for offenses against the United States, except in cases of impeachment;[33] and
>
> Article II, Section 4:
> The President, Vice President and all civil Officers of the United States, shall be removed from Office on Impeachment for, and Conviction of, Treason, Bribery, or other high Crimes and Misdemeanors.[34]

1. The Text And Structure Of The Articles Discussing Impeachment Do Not Grant To the Senate the Authority Over A Former President.

As is evident from our Constitution's plain text, Article II limits impeachment to current officials: "The President, Vice President and all civil Officers of the United States, shall be removed from Office on Impeachment for, and Conviction of, Treason, Bribery, or other high Crimes and Misdemeanors." As Alexis de Tocqueville wrote, impeachment was designed to

31 U.S. Const, art.1, § 2, cl. 5.

32 U.S. Const. art. 1, §3, cl. 6 and 7.

33 U.S. Const. art 2, § 2.

34 U.S. Const. art 2, § 4.

deprive a political actor "of the authority he has used to amiss."[35] In this instance, however, the Senate is being asked to do something patently ridiculous: try a private citizen in a process that is designed to remove him from an office *that he no longer holds*.

(a) The Impeachment of a Former President, A Private Citizen, Constitutes An Illegal Bill Of Attainder.

An impeachment trial of Mr. Trump held before the Senate would be nothing more nor less than the trial of a private citizen by a legislative body. An impeachment trial by the Senate of a private citizen violates Article I, Section 9 of the U.S. Constitution, which states that "[n]o bill of attainder . . . shall be passed."[36]

The Bill of Attainder, as this clause is known, prohibits Congress from enacting "a law that legislatively determines guilt and inflicts punishment upon an identifiable individual without provision of the protections of a judicial trial."[37] Simply put, "[a] bill of attainder is a legislative act which inflicts punishment without a judicial trial."[38] "The distinguishing characteristic of a bill of attainder is the substitution of legislative determination of guilt and legislative imposition of punishment for judicial finding and sentence."[39]

"[The Bill of Attainder Clause], and the separation of powers doctrine generally, reflect the Framers' concern that trial by a legislature lacks the safeguards necessary to prevent the abuse of

---

35 Katherine Shaw, *Impeachable Speech*, 70 Emory L.J. 1, 10 (2020), citing to ALEXIS DE TOCQUEVILLE, I DEMOCRACY IN AMERICA 101 (1838).

36 U.S. Const. art. I, § 9.

37 *Nixon v. Adm'r of Gen. Servs.*, 433 U.S. 425, 468 (1977).

38 *Cummings v. State of Missouri*, 71 U.S. 277, 323 (1866).

39 *United States v. Lovett*, 328 U.S. 303, 321-22 (1946) (Frankfurter, J., and Reed, J., concurring).

power."[40] As the Supreme Court explained in *United States v. Brown,*[41] "[t]he best available evidence, the writings of the architects of our constitutional system, indicate that the Bill of Attainder Clause was intended not as a narrow, technical (and therefore soon to be outmoded) prohibition, but rather as an implementation of the separation of powers, a general safeguard against legislative exercise of the judicial function, or more simply—trial by legislature."[42] The Bill of Attainder "reflected the Framers' belief that the Legislative Branch is not so well suited as politically independent judges and juries. . . "[43]

When the Senate undertakes an impeachment trial of a private citizen, it is acting as a judge and jury rather than a legislative body. And this is exactly the type of situation that the Bill of Attainder was meant to preclude. It is clear that disqualification from holding future office is a kind of punishment that is subject to the constitutional inhibition against the passage of bills of attainder, under which general designation bills of pains and penalties are included; in *Cummings, Ex parte Garland*, and *Brown*, the Supreme Court thrice struck down provisions that precluded support of the South or support of Communism from holding certain jobs as being in violation of this prohibition.[44] Thus the impeachment of a private citizen in order to disqualify them from holding office is an unconstitutional act constituting a Bill of Attainder.

---

40 *I.N.S. v. Chadha*, 462 U.S. 919, 962 (1983) (Powell, J., concurring opinion).

41 *United States v. Brown*, 381 U.S. 437, 442 (1965).

42 381 U.S. 437, 442 (1965).

43 *Id.* at 445.

44 *Cummings v. Missouri*, 71 U.S. 277 (1867)(noting that "[t]he deprivation of any rights, civil or political, previously enjoyed, may be punishment."); *Ex parte Garland*, 71 U.S. 333 (1866)(explaining that "exclusion from any of the professions or any of the ordinary avocations of life for past conduct can be regarded in no other light than as punishment for such conduct."); *see also Brown v. U.S.*, 381 U.S. 437, 458 (1965).

Moreover, this is the exact type of situation in which the fear would be great that some members of the Senate might be susceptible to acting in the haste the House did when it rushed through the Article of Impeachment in less than 48 hours, *i.e.*, acting hastily simply to appease the popular clamor of their political base.[45] As Chief Justice Marshall warned in *Fletcher v. Peck*,

> [I]t is not to be disguised that the framers of the constitution viewed, with some apprehension, the violent acts which might grow out of the feelings of the moment; and that the people of the United States, in adopting that instrument, have manifested a determination to shield themselves and their property from the effects of those sudden and strong passions to which men are exposed. The restrictions on the legislative power of the states are obviously founded in this sentiment; and the constitution of the United States contains what may be deemed a bill of rights for the people of each state. No state shall pass any bill of attainder. In this form the power of the legislature over the lives and fortunes of individuals is expressly restrained.[46]

2. The Constitution only gives the Senate Jurisdiction over the President, not the *former* President, of the United States.

One legal scholar described the simplicity of Article II's limitation, which House Managers try in vain to make seem inscrutable, in this way: "A half-grown boy reads in a newspaper that the President occupies the White House; if he would understand from that that all Ex-Presidents are in it together he would be considered a very unpromising lad."[47] That is the first reason why a former President cannot be impeached: he is not the President anymore.

As Professor Phillip Bobbit, one of the leading scholars on the impeachment process, and author of *Impeachment: A Handbook* (with Black, New Edition) (2018), recently argued:

---

45 *United States v. Brown*, 381 U.S. 437, 442 - 445 (1965).

46 *Fletcher v. Peck*, 10 U.S. 87, 137–38, 3 L. Ed. 162 (1810).

47 Brian C. Kalt, *The Constitutional Case for the Impeachability of Former Federal Officials: An Analysis of the Law, History, and Practice of Late Impeachment*, 6 Tex. Rev. L. & Pol. 13, 20 (2001).

> There is no authority granted to Congress to impeach and convict persons who are not "civil officers of the United States." It's as simple as that. But simplicity doesn't mean unimportance. Limiting Congress to its specified powers is a crucial element in the central idea of the U.S. Constitution: putting the state under law.[48]

Further textual support on this issue is evidenced by the Founders use of "shall" when identifying the penalty to be imposed, i.e. "...**shall** be removed from Office...." Justice Scalia once wrote, when the word "shall" can reasonably be understood as mandatory, it ought to be taken that way.[49] In 2007 the Supreme Court confirmed that

> The word `shall' generally indicates a command that admits of no discretion on the part of the person instructed to carry out the directive"); Black's Law Dictionary 1375 (6th ed. 1990) ("As used in statutes ... this word is generally imperative or mandatory").[50]

The text then is very clear: Conviction at an impeachment trial requires the possibility of a removal from office. Without that possibility, there cannot be a trial. In the civil law analogue, this case would be summarily dismissed under Federal Rules of Civil Procedure 12(b)(6), for "failure to state a claim upon which relief can be granted."[51]

The second reason a former President cannot be impeached follows logically from the first. The purpose of impeachment is to remove someone from office, and unequivocally, this impeachment trial is *not* about removing someone from office, as Mr. Trump left office on January 20, 2021. He is now, both factually and legally, a private citizen.

---

48 Bobbit, *Why the Senate Shouldn't Hold a Late Impeachment Trial,* Law Fare Blog (Jan. 27, 2021), https://www.lawfareblog.com/why-senate-shouldnt-hold-late-impeachment-trial#.

49 Scalia, Antonin; Garner, Bryan A. (2012). "11. Mandatory/Permissive Canon". *Reading Law: The Interpretation of Legal Texts* (Kindle ed.). St. Paul, MN: Thomson West. ISBN 978-0-314-27555-4.

50 *National Ass'n v. Defenders of Wildlife*, 551 U.S. 644, 661-62 (2007).

51 Fed. R. Civ. P. 12

House Managers have no authority to legally redefine "former Presidents" as "Presidents" for some constitutional provisions and not others. Would they accept a former President conducting foreign policy on behalf of the United States? Would they be content to have a "former President" nominate a Justice for a vacant seat on the Supreme Court? Of course not. That is why the term 'former President' is actually a term of art with legal ramifications, as evidenced by the Former Presidents Act (3 U.S.C. § 102 note), which states that:

> "(f)As used in this section, the term 'former President' means a person—
> "(1) who shall have held the office of President of the United States of America;
> "(2) whose service in such office shall have terminated other than by removal pursuant to section 4 of article II of the Constitution of the United States of America; and
> "(3) who does not then currently hold such office.

As it relates to the above definitional requirements, Mr. Trump has held the Office of President of the United States of America; his service was *not* terminated by removal pursuant to section 4 of article II of the Constitution (and even if this sham late impeachment were to result in a conviction, he *still* would not have been thus removed); and he does not currently hold such office. He is therefore *legally* in the separate category of 'former President' and is statutorily *not* the President of the United States referred to in the Impeachment Clauses of the Constitution. The text of the Constitution that provides only "[t]he President, Vice President and all Civil Officers of the United States, shall be removed from Office on Impeachment," supports the conclusion that the impeachment process applies only to officials in office.[52] This provision does not state "a" President or "a former" President, it unequivocally states "the" President. And when one refers to

---

[52] Harold J. Krent, *Can President Trump Be Impeached As Mr. Trump? Exploring the Temporal Dimension of Impeachments*, 95 Chi.-Kent L. Rev. 537, 540 (2020)(noting that RTILCE II "appears to limit impeachment of "officers" only when "removal" is possible, i.e., when the officer is still serving.")

"the" President, the reference is clearly to the current President. The text of the Constitution simply does not contain language allowing for the impeachment of a former President and does not address "late impeachments," i.e., an impeachment of a former officer.[53] Any inference from British practice about former officials is therefore a nullity because they *would* impeach private citizens, and our Framers decided *not* to do that. We chose not to remain British after all.

3. The Founders Knowingly Did Not Extend The Power Of Impeachment To Former Officials.

The Founders clearly decided to purposefully limit the power of impeachment in this way. The concept of a "late impeachment" was in use at the time the Constitution was written, with Great Britain specifically allowing impeachment of former officials.[54] In fact, the British Parliament could, and did, impeach private citizens. The Framers could have explicitly included a provision allowing for the impeachment of a former President, but they did not. Instead, the Constitution was written to restrict impeachment to specific public officials: "*the* President, Vice President, and other civil officers."[55]

"There is little discussion in the historical record surrounding the framing and ratification of the Constitution that treats the precise question of whether a person no longer a civil officer can

---

53 As stated in a recent report from the Congressional Research Service on "The Impeachment and Trial of a Former President": "The Constitution does not directly address whether Congress may impeach and try a former President for actions taken while in office," and "the text is open to debate." Congressional Research Service "The Impeachment and Trial of a Former President" https://crsreports.congress.gov/product/pdf/LSB/LSB10565 (Jan. 15, 2021).

54 Kalt at 25-26 (discussing state constitutions which specifically provided for late impeachments and quoting several constitutions which specifically provided for impeachment of an official "when he is out of office" or "either when in office, or after his resignation, or removal").

55 As argued by Jeremiah S. Black during Senator William Blount's impeachment: "A half-grown boy reads in a newspaper that *the* President occupies the White House; if he would understand from that that all Ex-Presidents are in it together he would be considered a very unpromising lad." 3 Hinds *Precedents of the House of Representatives*, § 2007 at 314 (1907). https://www.govinfo.gov/collection/precedents-of-the-house?path=/GPO/Precedents%20of%20the%20U.S.%20House%20of%20Representatives

be impeached—and in light of the clarity of the text, this is hardly surprising."[56] The text is also doubly clear given the clarity of available models in some of the United States themselves that *did* allow for late impeachments to take place.[57]

While the House Managers cite to some non-binding statements from John Quincy Adams about the possibility of late impeachment (in a case that did not even end with an impeachment) there is equal and perhaps even more on the scant record that would weigh against it. For example, as Professor Brian Kalt details, in multiple places Alexander "Hamilton seemed to believe that removal was a required component of the impeachment penalty, which suggests that he viewed

---

56 Bobbit, *supra.* https://www.lawfareblog.com/why-senate-shouldnt-hold-late-impeachment-trial

57 For example, the state Constitution of Vermont (7/1777) provides "the General Assembly [sic] of the Representatives of the Freemen of Vermont . . . may . . . impeach State criminals. Every officer of State, whether judicial or executive, shall be liable to be impeached by the General Assembly, either when in office, **or after his resignation, or removal** for mal-administration . . . Vt. Const. of 1777, ch. 2, § 20; or Pennsylvania (9/1776): "The general assembly of the representatives of the freemen of Pennsylvania . . . may . . . impeach state criminals. Every officer of state, whether judicial or executive, shall be liable to be impeached by the general assembly, either when in office, or after his resignation, or removal for mal-administration . . . .Pa. Const. of 1776, ch. II, §22.

As Brian Kalt explains, ideas like requiring a two-thirds majority to convict in the Senate are not self-evident, which is why the Framers took the time to spell them out. Late impeachment, so the argument goes, which is also not self-evident, would have also required specification if the Framers wished to include it as a possibility. Kalt at 37, see also *id* at fn. 441:

> See N.J. Const. of 1844, art. V, §11 ("The governor and all other officers under this State shall be liable to impeachment for misdemeanor in office, during their continuance in office, and for two years thereafter.") (emphasis added); Proceedings of the New Jersey State Constitutional Convention of 1844, at 600 (New Jersey Writers' Project ed., 1942) (chronicling last-minute addition of late impeachment provision); see also N.J. Const. art. VII, §3, cl. 1 ("The Governor and all other State officers, while in office and for two years thereafter, shall be liable to impeachment for misdemeanor committed during their respective continuance in office.").

Clearly late impeachment was something that people thought about, talked about, and wrote about, *if* they wanted to include it in their laws.

late impeachment as impossible."[58] In The Federalist No. 39, Madison wrote that the President of the United States is impeachable *at any time during his continuance in office*.[59] (Emphasis added).[60]

---

[58] Kalt at 43.

[59] Kalt at 50, citing The Federalist No. 39, at 397 (James Madison) (Clinton Rossiter ed., 1961). Kalt also notes that the other discussions of impeachment in The Federalist concerned removability, which buttresses the argument that impeachment was intended for sitting officers. *Id.* at 51.

[60] Other states, like Georgia *had* late impeachment clauses up to a point and then and removed them. Kalt quotes the Georgia committee's discussion at length, noting that their consideration is very illuminating as an example of commonsense intuitions about the idea of a late impeachment:

> DR. PYLES: May I raise another question? What about this ". . . against all persons who shall have been . . . ." What's the point? . . This is highly confusing if you say ". . . shall have been in office . . . ." That's almost ex post facto or something.
> MR. CLARK: How can you impeach somebody who's not in office[?]
> DR. PYLES: Yeah. Or why. We've got criminal provisions, law, civil law.
> MR. CLARK: Any understandable background for that, that phraseology, "shall have been" ?
> CHAIRMAN SWEENEY: No.. . .
> MR. TIDWELL: If you look further into what you can do, the consequences are, he cannot hold office again. That might shed some light on that. . ..
> MR. HILL: . . . Now a person could leave office and two or three years later something is found out about that person that would be serious enough to warrant an impeachment trial so that he or she could never hold office again. . . . I don't think the language was happenstance, I think it was intended to cover both people in office and former officeholders.
> MR. CLARK: . . . [I]mpeachment is to put that person out of office, it seems to me, and the idea if he has committed some malfeasance or violation, that there would be criminal support, this falls into court action rather than the ponderous procedure of an impeachment. I just can't see it ever coming about . . . it clutters up again and adds questions to the Constitution that is just not necessary.
> MS. RYSTROM: I agree with you....
> DR. PYLES: I actually think the impeachment provision serves as a deterrent or maybe a threat against an officer, whether it will ever be carried out or not, the fact that it could be carried out is a pretty viable threat it would seem to me to an individual before he continued to persist in whatever it was that would be heinous enough to warrant impeachment.
> CHAIRMAN SWEENEY: Especially if he knows that it may come up after he leaves office.
> MR CLARK: . . . I don't think it's enough--it's not important enough to quibble about. I don't think it's likely to come up again, so I would be

Interestingly, where the Constitution refers to "the President" in Article 1, Section 3 and gives protocols for impeachment, such as "when the President of the United States is tried [in the Senate], the Chief Justice shall preside," the Senate reads this as applicable to the impeachment trial only of the current sitting President. Yet, under the House Managers' theory, they urge the Senate to read the constitutional provision that specifies "the President" is subject to impeachment to include a former President.[61]

4. Historical Precedents

(a) The Failed Attempts to Impeach Senator William Blount and Secretary of War William Belknap

The House Managers suggests there is "congressional precedent" for impeaching a former President in the impeachment cases of Senator William Blount and Secretary of War William Belknap. These two cases are actually inapposite and do not provide any binding precedential authority for impeaching a former President. .

In 1797, United States Senator William Blount of Tennessee faced allegations of conspiring to help Great Britain seize Spanish-controlled areas in Florida and what is now Louisiana as part of a scheme to pay off debts incurred from land speculation. Blount was expelled

---

> opposed to leaving the wording in there, I don't think it serves any protective purpose at all.
> CHAIRMAN SWEENEY: Well, is there a motion to drop it?. . .
> DR. PYLES: I so move.. . .
> CHAIRMAN SWEENEY: All in favor?
> MS. RYSTROM: I was getting convinced on the other side as this discussion went on.
> CHAIRMAN SWEENEY: Four [out of seven committee members present] in favor of dropping the language.

Kalt at 109-11, quoting from 2 State of Georgia Select Committee on Constitutional Revision, Transcript of Meetings, 1977-1981, Committee to Revise Article III, Oct. 29, 1979, at 29-30 (stating subcommittee's understanding that leaving office "obviate[s] the need for an impeachment proceeding."). Virginia removed late impeachment in 1830. See Kalt at 114, citing to Va. Const. of 1830, art. III, §13.

[61] House Trial Memo. at 48-50.

by the Senate prior to his impeachment proceedings in 1798, he therefore argued that he was not subject to trial and refused to appear. Specifically, Blount argued that Senators or members of Congress could not be impeached, but only expelled by their respective chamber, and, even if Senators *could* be impeached, ex-Senators could not.

"In a close vote, the Senate defeated a resolution asserting Blount was an impeachable civil officer. But the debate around this vote, and the text of the resolution, do not make clear whether the resolution was rejected because it was felt that a senator was not "a civil officer" or whether, having been expelled, Blount ceased to be impeachable."[62] Therefore the case has little or no precedential value supporting a late impeachment.

In 1876, Belknap, Secretary of War under President Ulysses S. Grant, was investigated by the House for corruption. Belknap had accepted over $20,000 in kickbacks for the appointment of an associate to a lucrative military trading post at Fort Sill.[63] However, on March 2, 1876, after the House had taken up the issue but before the House voted on his impeachment, Grant accepted Belknap's resignation[64] – apparently just minutes before the House was set to vote.[65] Despite Belknap's resignation, the House voted to impeach him anyway. The issue of whether an officer who had resigned could be impeached was heavily debated from May15 to May 29th, but

62 *Id.*

63 United State Senate.gov https://www.senate.gov/artandhistory/history/minute/War_Secretarys_Impeachment_Trial.htm).

64 Of course the Belknap case is arguably different than Mr. Trump's because Mr. Trump did *not* try and escape a trial by resignation; this entire constitutional problem was created by the Democratic leadership that chose to wait until after his term had naturally expired.

65 *Id.*

ultimately the Senate voted 37-29 that it had the power to hold an impeachment trial for a former officeholder and proceeded to have a trial.[66]

On August 1, 1876, Belknap was acquitted because less than 2/3 of the Senate voted for impeachment.[67] While historical accounts suggest that few senators believed Belknap was innocent, the majority of those voting to acquit him did so **because they did not think the Senate had jurisdiction to convict someone who was no longer in office.**[68]

---

66 *Id.*

67 *Id.*

68 3 Hinds *Precedents of the House of Representatives*, § 2467 (1907):

> An analysis of the reasons given with the votes shows that of those voting ''guilty,'' 2 believed that the Senate had no jurisdiction, but gave their verdict in good faith, since by vote jurisdiction had been assumed. Of those voting ''not guilty,''3 announced that they did so on the evidence, while 22 announced that they voted not guilty because they believed the Senate had no jurisdiction. One Senator stated that he declined to vote because he believed they did not have jurisdiction.

As Alan Dershowitz framed this case and its relative import:

> No former official has ever been convicted by the Senate, and only one has been impeached. Secretary of War William W. Belknap was indisputably guilty of numerous impeachable offences, to which he confessed as he resigned his office hours before the House unanimously impeached him in 1876. The Senate voted in favor of a procedural motion affirming its jurisdiction to try Belknap's impeachment. But two dozen senators who believed he was guilty voted to acquit on jurisdictional grounds. A close vote nearly a century and a half ago doesn't establish a binding precedent.

Alan Dershowitz, *Senate Should Dismiss Article Impeachment Since Trump is Now Private Citizen,* The Hill (Jan. 21, 2021), https://thehill.com/homenews/media/535261-dershowitz-senate-should-dismiss-article-impeachment-since-trump-is-now.

There are also other recent precedents, in 1926 and 2009, in which judges resigned having been impeached, after which the House then petitioned the Senate to withdraw the indictment. See Bobbit, *supra.*, https://www.lawfareblog.com/why-senate-shouldnt-hold-late-impeachment-trial.

Significantly, neither Belknap nor Blount received the required two-thirds majority of the Senate and were acquitted so their proceedings provide no binding precedent establishing the Senate's jurisdiction to convict former officials of impeachment. "These cases cannot be read as foreclosing an argument that they never dealt with."[69] This is critically important because the burden of proof applies to both jurisdictional and substantive elements: "[T]he substantive elements of a federal statute describe the evil Congress seeks to prevent; the jurisdictional element connects the law to one of Congress's enumerated powers, thus establishing legislative authority. Both kinds of elements must be proved to a jury beyond a reasonable doubt; and because that is so, both may play a real role in a criminal case."[70] With impeachments, jurisdiction and guilt must be found by a two-thirds majority. Neither case established jurisdiction by the required two-thirds' majority. These two instances present, at best, an example of hypothetical jurisdiction.[71] It is also

---

69 *Waters v. Churchill*, 511 U.S. 661, 678, 114 S. Ct. 1878, 1889 (1994)(plurality). Furthermore, a court "is not bound by prior *sub silentio* holdings when a subsequent case finally brings the jurisdictional issue before us." *Will v. Michigan Dep't of State Police*, 491 U.S. 58, 63, n.4 (1989)(Court's alterations omitted) quoting *Hagans v. Lavine*, 415 U.S. 528, 535, n.5 (1977).

70 *Torres v. Lynch,* 136 S. Ct. 1619, 1630 (2016) (citations omitted).

71 *Steel Co. v. Citizens for a Better Env't*, 523 U.S. 83, 101-02, 118 S. Ct. 1003, 1016 (1998). The *Steel* Court discussed the threshold inquiry into jurisdiction noting contested questions of law could not be resolved when jurisdiction was in doubt:

> Hypothetical jurisdiction produces nothing more than a hypothetical judgment -- which comes to the same thing as an advisory opinion, disapproved by this Court from the beginning. *Muskrat v. United States*, 219 U.S. 346, 362, 55 L. Ed. 246, 31 S. Ct. 250 (1911); *Hayburn's Case*, 2 U.S. 409, 2 Dall. 409, 1 L. Ed. 436 (1792). Much more than legal niceties are at stake here. The statutory and (especially) constitutional elements of jurisdiction are an essential ingredient of separation and equilibration of powers, restraining the courts from acting at certain times, and even restraining them from acting permanently regarding certain subjects. *See United States v. Richardson*, 418 U.S. 166, 179, 41 L. Ed. 2d 678, 94 S. Ct. 2940 (1974); *Schlesinger v. Reservists Comm. to Stop the War*, 418 U.S. 208, 227, 41 L. Ed. 2d 706, 94 S. Ct. 2925 (1974). For a court to pronounce upon the meaning or the constitutionality of a state or federal

worth noting that neither of those cases dealt with a President, with his unique status in the Constitution, and with the clear definitional limits that apply to him and not to others.

(b) More Recent Impeachment Proceedings

In the past, Congress has acknowledged and exercised its duty to not impeach when an official is no longer in office. In the case involving the impeachment of President Richard M. Nixon, Congress decided not to impeach because he resigned from office. "[A]s a practical matter… the resignation of an official about to be impeached generally puts an end to impeachment proceedings because the primary objective—removal from office—has been accomplished." [72]

In May 1974, the House Judiciary Committee began formal impeachment hearings against President Nixon in regard to the Watergate scandal, and, on July 27, 1974, the House Judiciary Committee approved three articles of impeachment and reported them to the full House for consideration. Knowing that he was about to be impeached in the House and convicted in the Senate, Nixon resigned on August 8, 1974. The House officially ended the impeachment process against him on August 20, 1974, by accepting the committee's report, but deciding not to further advance impeachment proceedings.

As professor Bobbitt explained: "Why didn't they go ahead and impeach him when he resigned? The answer is they didn't believe that they had the authority to impeach someone who could not be removed, someone who was no longer, as the [constitutional] text requires, a 'civil officer' of the United States."[73] A memo from the Office of Legal Counsel at the time reached a

---

law when it has no jurisdiction to do so is, by very definition, for a court to act ultra vires.

[72] *House Practice: A Guide to the Rules, Precedents and Procedures of the House*, Chap. 27 Impeachment § 2 at 604-05.

[73] Interview with Columbia Law professor Philip Bobbitt, co-author of <u>Impeachment: A Handbook</u> (<u>https://www.npr.org/2021/01/18/957866252/can-the-senate-try-an-ex-president</u>).

very similar conclusion "[a]s a practical matter, if the President should resign, this would probably result in termination of impeachment proceedings."[74]

(c) State Courts Have Rejected Claims Similar To Those Made By The House Managers In Similar Late Impeachment Matters.

While the Supreme Court has not yet addressed the question of a late impeachment, some state courts have. In *State v. Hill*, the Supreme Court of Nebraska dealt with the exact same substantive question facing the Senate now, on almost identical Constitutional language. They addressed head on and dismissed the same claims that the House Managers now make. First, they started with the plain meaning of the word *officer* at issue:

> It is urged by counsel for the managers that ex–officers are liable to impeachment for official misdemeanors committed while in office; that jurisdiction attaches immediately upon the commission of an impeachable offense; and that the expiration of the official term does not deprive the legislature of the power to impeach, or the court to try. It cannot be said that there is any provision of the constitution which expressly confers the authority to impeach a person after he is out of office; while section 5, already quoted, designates the persons who may be impeached as "all civil officers of this state." This language is unambiguous. It means existing officers,—persons in office at the time they are impeached. Ex–officials are not civil officers within the meaning of the constitution. Jurisdiction to impeach attaches at the time the offense is committed, and continues during the time the offender remains in office, but no longer.[75]

Then the Court proceeded to address the question of disqualification as a separate remedial punishment:

> The necessary implication of the provisions in section 14, art. 3, of the constitution, that "judgment in cases of impeachment shall not extend further than removal from office and disqualification to hold

---

[74] U.S. Department of Justice, *Legal Aspects of Impeachment: An Overview, Volumes 1-5,* https://books.google.com/books?id=tHyQAAAAMAAJ&printsec=frontcover&source=gbs_ge_summary_r&cad=0#v=onepage&q&f=false.

[75] *State v. Hill*, 55 N.W. 794, 796 (Neb. 1893).

and enjoy any office of honor, profit, or trust in this state," is that the offending party must be in office at the time the impeachment proceedings are commenced. In case of impeachment, either one of two judgments can be pronounced, namely, removal from office, or removal and disqualification to hold office. It is obvious that there can be no judgment of removal where the party was not an officer when impeached. It is claimed by counsel for the managers, as we understand their argument, that a judgment of disqualification can be entered without a judgment of removal. All will concede that disqualification to hold office is a punishment much greater than removal; so that, if the construction contended for by counsel is the true one, then, in case the person impeached is out of office, he is liable to a more severe penalty than might have been inflicted upon him had he been impeached before he went out of office. We cannot believe that the members of the convention who framed the constitution so intended. Judge Story, in discussing the question whether a person can be impeached after he has ceased to hold office, at section 803 says: "As it is declared in one clause of the constitution that judgment in cases of impeachment shall not extend further than a removal from office, and disqualification to hold any office of honor, trust, or profit under the United States, and in another clause, that the 'president, vice president, and all civil officers of the United States shall be removed from office on impeachment for, and conviction of, treason, bribery, or other high crimes or misdemeanors,' it would seem to follow that the senate, on the conviction, were bound in all cases to enter a judgment of removal from office, though it has a discretion as to inflicting the punishment of disqualification. If, then, there must be a judgment of removal from office, it would seem to follow that the constitution contemplated that the party was still in office at the time of impeachment. If he was not, his offense was still liable to be tried and punished in the ordinary tribunals of justice. And it might be argued, with some force, that it would be a vain exercise of authority to try a delinquent for an impeachable offense, when the most important object for which the remedy was given was no longer necessary or attainable; and, although a judgment of disqualification might still be pronounced, the language of the constitution may create some doubt whether it can be pronounced without being coupled with a removal from office." [76]

[76] *Id.* at 796-97. Next the Court "rejected the British cases of Hastings and Melville as irrelevant given the broader scope of English impeachment… [and] rejected the Belknap precedent because of the weakness of the Senate's majority and also because, unlike Belknap, Benton and Hill were out of office from the natural expiration of their terms." Kalt, at 117; see also *id.* at fn. 454: describing how "in a case decided the same day, the court dismissed another late impeachment on different grounds, while noting its argument in Hill. *State v. Leese*, 55 N.W. 798, 799 (Neb. 1893) (citing Hill and pointing out that the legislature had no power to impeach Leese because he had been out of office for two years)."

The most recent state court opinion on late impeachment is *Smith v. Brantley*,[77] a Florida case from 1981 that also declared late impeachment unacceptable. The Florida Supreme Court held that:

> officers are officers; ex-officers, who could not be suspended or removed from office, are not. The court thus was making the linguistic argument that "officer" meant "sitting officer" and the functional argument that "the primary and dominant purpose of impeachment in Florida is removal of an officeholder from office. Once an officer has resigned, this purpose is fulfilled, the court said, and the mere possibility of disqualification from future office does not change the fact that the main purpose of the process has been achieved. The court considered Blount, Belknap, and Ferguson, but argued that in each case the resignation did not occur until impeachment proceedings had begun.[78]

B. Congress' Power To Impose Penalties Upon Conviction Of Impeachment Is Limited to Removal, And (Not Or) Disqualification.

The Constitution grants Congress only the power to remove a person's right to run for office when it is part of the process of removal from office. Article II, Section 4, of the Constitution states that the only purpose of an impeachment is whether "the President, Vice president and all civil Officers of the United States, shall be removed from office." The only purpose of impeachment is to remove the President, Vice-President, and civil officers from office. When a President is no longer in office, the objective of an impeachment ceases.[79]

---

77 *Smith v. Brantley*, 400 So. 2d 443 (Fla. 1981)

78 Kalt at 120-121.

79 Kalt at 66, *see also* fn. 112:

> *See, e.g.*, 14 Annals of Cong. 430-31 (1805) (speech of Luther Martin in impeachment trial of Justice Samuel Chase) ("The President, Vice President, and other civil officers can only be impeached.... In the first article, section the third, of the Constitution, it is declared that, judgment in all cases of impeachment, shall not extend further than removal from office, and disqualification to hold any office of honor, trust, or profit,

This impeachment trial is being pursued solely to preclude Mr. Trump, a private citizen, from holding any future office. However, the Constitution does not provide for the impeachment of a private citizen who is not in office. Further, the Constitution only grants the Senate the additional power to remove a person's right to run for office as *part* of the process of removal from office.[80] When a person ceases to hold an office, he immediately becomes a private citizen, impervious to removal, and therefore to impeachment and trial by the Senate.

As Professor Harold Krent has noted, "although the Impeachment Clause in Article I states that the penalty for impeachment shall not extend beyond removal and disqualification from office, that clause reads as a limit on what type of punishment can be meted rather than addressing "when." The Framers presumably were signaling the change from the British practice under which additional penalties were possible. There is no language in the Constitution suggesting that the impeachment authority is continuous."[81]

This idea was perhaps best expressed by Supreme Court Justice Joseph Story, in his influential three volume treatise *Commentaries on the Constitution of the United States*:

> **§ 801.** As it is declared in one clause of the constitution, that "judgment, in cases of impeachment, shall not extend further, than a removal from office, and disqualification to hold any office of honour, trust, or profit, under the United States;" and in another clause, that "the president, vice president, and all civil officers of the United States, shall be removed from office on impeachment for, and conviction of, treason, bribery, or other high crimes or misdemeanors;" it would seem to follow, that the senate, on the

> under the United States. This clearly evinces, that no persons but those who hold offices are liable to impeachment.

[80] Dershowitz, *No, You can't try an Impeached Former President,* Wall Street Journal (Jan. 21, 2021),*https://www.wsj.com/articles/no-you-cant-try-an-impeached-former-president-11611167113?mod=article_inline* (contrasting the word "and" with the word "or.")

[81] Harold J. Krent, *Can President Trump Be Impeached As Mr. Trump? Exploring the Temporal Dimension of Impeachments*, 95 Chi.-Kent L. Rev. 537, 542 (2020).

> conviction, were bound, in all cases, to enter a judgment of removal from office, though it has a discretion, as to inflicting the punishment of disqualification. If, then, there must be a judgment of removal from office, it would seem to follow, that the constitution contemplated, that the party was still in office at the time of the impeachment. If he was not, his offence was still liable to be tried and punished in the ordinary tribunals of justice. And it might be argued with some force, that it would be a vain exercise of authority to try a delinquent for an impeachable offence, when the most important object, for which the remedy was given, was no longer necessary, or attainable. And although a judgment of disqualification might still be pronounced, the language of the constitution may create some doubt, whether it can be pronounced without being coupled with a removal from office.[82]

The House Managers' failure to grasp this concept is evident from their misplaced reliance on this language to try and create a work-around of a problem of their own making, i.e. Mr. Trump was no longer President at the time the House filed the Article of Impeachment in the Senate. Instead, their argument further demonstrates the point that Mr. Trump could not be removed from office (because his term ended), the condition precedent to any further penalty. As Professor Alan Dershowitz explained:

> The Constitution is clear: "The president . . . shall be removed from office on impeachment . . . and conviction"—not by the expiration of his term before the impeachment process is complete. It also mandates that "judgment in cases of impeachment shall not extend further than to removal and disqualification"—not *or* disqualification.[83]

---

82 Justice Joseph Story, *Commentaries on the Constitution of the United States* at § 801.

83 Alan Dershowitz, *No, You can't try an Impeached Former President,* Wall Street Journal, (Jan. 21, 2021), *https://www.wsj.com/articles/no-you-cant-try-an-impeached-former-president-11611167113?mod=article_inline*

Other scholars have forcefully rejected the failed interpretation the House Managers try to advance in an effort to salvage this doomed impeachment by spelling out the unstated assumptions inherent in their position:

> by this logic a president could be disqualified from holding office without being removed, an obvious absurdity. This argument asserts that, because the Senate could, by a simple majority, disqualify a person impeached and convicted under Article II, it would thwart the operation of Article I, Clause 7's list of permissible punishments to let the convicted former officer go free. Were it otherwise, an officer could avoid removal and disqualification by simply resigning. This circular argument assumes the truth of the proposition that a person no longer in office can be impeached in the first place and then infers from this assumption that such a power should not be frustrated. It is not compatible with Article II, which provides the sole constitutional grounds for trial in the Senate on the basis of which impeachment penalties can be imposed: the commission of bribery, treason, or other high crimes and misdemeanors by a civil officer leading to his removal. It relies instead on a tortured inference from Article I, whose text says nothing about who can be impeached or on what grounds. In an effort to salvage the penalty of disqualification where an official has been impeached while in office but has resigned, advocates for this view would have the Senate convict a person no longer in office, inventing a new basis for conviction beyond that provided in Article II.[84]

The Constitution does not provide for an impeachment of someone who is not in office as a means to an end resulting in only disqualification – and for good reason. As Alexander Hamilton wrote:

> Nothing is more common than for a free people, in times of heat and violence, to gratify momentary passions by letting into the government principles and precedents which afterwards prove fatal to themselves. Of this kind is the doctrine of disqualification, disfranchisement, and banishment by acts of the legislature. The dangerous consequences of this power are manifest. If the legislature can disfranchise any number of citizens at pleasure by general descriptions, it may soon confine all the votes to a small number of partisans, and establish an aristocracy or an oligarchy; if it may banish at discretion all those whom particular circumstances

[84] Bobbit, *supra.*, https://www.lawfareblog.com/why-senate-shouldnt-hold-late-impeachment-trial

> render obnoxious, without hearing or trial, no man can be safe, nor know when he may be the innocent victim of a prevailing faction. The name of liberty applied to such a government would be a mockery of common sense.[85]

The House Managers put a lot of misplaced importance onto the fact that Article I Section 7 contains a clause reminding Congress of its own limitations, namely that after a conviction and removal, the only other penalty Congress can impose is disqualification. "Judgment in Cases of Impeachment shall not extend further than to removal from Office, and disqualification to hold and enjoy any Office of honor," does *not* mean that disqualification is a separate or alternative form of punishment entirely. Disqualification from future office is simply an additional discretionary penalty that the Senate may impose once it has determined the original purpose of the impeachment, removal, is proper. Disqualification, however, is not the purpose of an impeachment proceeding, and it is not available simply to disqualify a former public officer from future officeholding.

But that is not all. The House Managers are not content to argue that an officer who is impeached while in office can then be tried after they leave office;[86] the House Managers dig in further and claim that a person can be impeached at any time after they leave office.[87] The absence of a statute of limitations suggests that process is confined to present office holders: "A federal

---

[85] Hamilton, A., *A Letter from Phocion to the Considerate Citizens of New York* (January 27, 1784), https://founders.archives.gov/documents/Hamilton/01-03-02-0314#ARHN-01-03-02-0314-fn-0001 .

[86] Although the same textual inferences against such proceedings would apply, especially because there *were* states that *did* allow for just that: some states, there is an arguable textual and structural basis for drawing a distinction between the stages of impeachment. For instance, Nebraska state law provided: "An impeachment of any state officer shall be tried, notwithstanding such officer may have resigned his office, or his term of office has expired." This language more easily supports the notion that impeachment is limited to sitting officers but that trial is not. Kalt at 76 citing to *State v. Hill*, 55 N.W. at 798 (quoting Neb. Comp. Stat. ch. 19, § 8 (1891)).

[87] House Trial Memo at 2.

cause of action 'brought at any distance of time' would be 'utterly repugnant to the genius of our laws.'"[88]

In addition, at any given moment in time "[t]he majority party could threaten to impeach former officeholders of the minority party unless support is forthcoming on a particular appropriations or other bill. In other words, the ongoing threat of impeachment might distort law-making... and, as a functional matter, might interfere with the balance of powers otherwise prescribed in the Constitution."[89]

This is a dangerous slippery slope that the Senate should be careful to avoid. Were it otherwise, a future House could impeach former Vice President Biden for his obstruction of justice in setting up the Russia hoax circa 2016. While he could not be removed from the Vice Presidency because his term ended in 2017, he could be barred from holding future office. The same flawed logic the House Managers advance could apply to former Secretary of State Clinton for her violations of 18 U.S.C § 793. Impeachment cannot and should not be allowed to devolve into a political weapon.

Setting aside the clear meaning of the text, the House Managers argument about the need for late impeachment with disqualification upon conviction to serve as a deterrence for Presidential wrongdoing is also unfounded. A President who left office is not in any way above the law; as the Constitution states he or she is like any other citizen and can be tried in a court of law. From a political standpoint as well, an officer who has left office and is seeking to return faces the *ultimate*

---

88 *Wilson v. Garcia*, 471 U.S. 261, 271, 105 S. Ct. 1938, 1944 (1985) (quoting *Adams v. Woods*, 6 U.S. (2 Cranch) 336, 342 (1805)), abrogated in part on other grounds, Pub. L. No. 101-650, Title III, § 313(a), 104 Stat. 5089, 5114-5115 (1990).

89 *Id. See also*, Laurent Sacharoff, *Former Presidents and Executive Privilege*, 88 Tex. L. Rev. 301, 315 (2009), noting that Congress "cannot impeach a former President."

political check even without disqualification- the electorate. It is almost laughable that the House Managers, who spent four years pretending that Mr. Trump was completely ineffective and illegitimate, are now so worried that he might win again that they seek to illegally impair him.

Accordingly, the Senate does not have the power to try a former President and should dismiss the Article of Impeachment. Any other outcome would do profound and lasting damage to the institution of the Presidency. In this political climate we have seen the statues and monuments of former Presidents attacked because the values of their times were not in line with supposed modern sensibilities; if this impeachment of a former President is allowed to go forward, we could expect dozens more to follow from potentially both sides of the aisle, depending on which party happens to be in the majority.

> Future Congresses would judge the conduct of Presidents and other civil officers from the perspective of a different political and social milieu. From the vantage point of subsequent Congresses, President Clinton may have had a #MeToo problem; President Lyndon Johnson evidently spoke disparagingly about race; President George W. Bush lied to the public about domestic surveillance, and so on. And, although historical judgment may, at times, be healthy, the power of impeachment comes with tangible penalties.[90]

It is also true that, even if the Senate were to convict him without jurisdiction, such a decision would not go unchallenged. If Mr. Trump decides to run again, any non-binding 'disqualification' from an unauthorized Senate vote could and would be challenged in a court of law.[91] As scholars across the spectrum have agreed, certain aspects of impeachment *are* justiciable.

---

[90] Harold J. Krent, *Can President Trump Be Impeached As Mr. Trump? Exploring the Temporal Dimension of Impeachments*, 95 Chi.-Kent L. Rev. 537, 546 (2020).

[91] Christopher Silvester, *Beware the bill of attainder*, The Critic (Jan. 29, 2021), https://thecritic.co.uk/beware-the-bill-of-attainder/

For example, if, in a case like this, where "the President was tried by someone other than the Chief Justice,"[92] a Court would be likely to hear the matter on review.[93]

C. The Article of Impeachment Violates Mr. Trump's First Amendment Rights

Aside from the fact that it does not constitute a crime, let alone a high crime or misdemeanor, President Trump's speech at the January 6, 2021 event fell well within the norms of political speech that is protected by the First Amendment, and to try him for that would be to

---

[92] Josh Blackman, *What happens if the Chief Justice cannot serve at the Presidential impeachment trial?*, The Volokh Conspiracy (Nov. 25, 2019), https://reason.com/volokh/2019/11/25/what-happens-if-the-chief-justice-cannot-serve-at-the-presidential-impeachment-trial/.

[93] As Adam Liptak described it in the NY Times;

> Still, the 1993 decision did appear to leave open a possible role for the court were the Senate to violate what Chief Justice Rehnquist wrote were "the three very specific requirements" in the constitutional text — "that the Senate's members must be under oath or affirmation, that a two-thirds vote is required to convict and that the chief justice presides when the president is tried."
> When the case was argued, he asked the government's lawyer, Solicitor General Ken Starr, whether violations of those provisions could be challenged in court. (Mr. Starr would go on to investigate Mr. Clinton as independent counsel and to prepare the report that led to his impeachment.)
> **For instance, Chief Justice Rehnquist asked, what would happen if the chief justice died and Congress "created the office of vice chief justice?"**
> "We're going to let him preside," the chief justice said, sketching out the Senate's reasoning, "because it would just be catastrophic to wait for the appointment of a chief justice while this impeachment is pending."
> "Can the Senate not do that because of the specific language 'the chief justice shall preside'?" Chief Justice Rehnquist asked. "Would that action by the Senate, followed by the presiding by the vice chief justice, be judicially reviewable?"
> "I have to admit," Mr. Starr said, with apparent reluctance, that the answer was yes.

Adam Liptak, *Can Trump Challenge His Impeachment in the Supreme Court*, New York Times (Dec. 17, 2019), https://www.nytimes.com/2019/11/25/us/trump-impeachment-supreme-court.html.

do a grave injustice to the freedom of speech in this country.[94] Perhaps in realization that Mr. Trump's speech was clearly within the bounds the protections afforded by the First Amendment, the House Managers attempt to erect artificial roadblocks to prevent the Senate from even considering First Amendment principles in these impeachment proceedings. These efforts – as fully discussed below – are complete sophistry that should be rejected by the Senators, who are duty bound to consider and apply the First Amendment.

1. The Senate Cannot Disregard the First Amendment and the Supreme Court's Long-Established Free Speech Jurisprudence

The House Managers' Trial Memorandum expressly advocates for the Senate to disregard First Amendment principles, stating "the First Amendment does not apply *at all* to an impeachment proceeding."[95] In doing so, the House Managers shockingly invite Senators to violate their own oaths to uphold the Constitution and the bedrock principle—established over two hundred years ago—that the Supreme Court is the final arbiter of whether Congressional acts are consistent with the Constitution.[96] There is no actual precedent for this confounding precept offered in the House Managers' Brief—the Managers astonishingly cite to a few recent internet *blogs*.[97]

The First Amendment is widely understood as prohibiting Congress from "abridging the freedom of speech; or the right of people peaceably to assemble" in all aspects of state action in

---

94 Miranda Devine, *Facebook's squad of though police: Devine,* https://nypost.com/2021/01/31/facebooks-squad-of-thought-police-devine/; *see also* Tammy Bruce, *The new thought police: Inside the left's assault on free speech and free minds* (Crown, 2010).

95 House Trial Memo. at 45.

96 *Marbury v. Madison*, 5 U.S. 137 (1803) ("It is emphatically the province and duty of the Judicial Department to say what the law is.")

97 Mem. of U.S. House of Rep. at 45 n.201.

all three branches of government.[98] Congress may not take action that would "abridge the freedom of speech." Indeed, Senators take an Oath of Office, which includes an oath to "support and defend the Constitution of the United States . . . ."[99] The Constitution, of course, includes the Bill of Rights, including the First Amendment. This means, inevitably, that Senators cannot do what the House Managers urge: the Senate cannot blithely cast aside the First Amendment and the Supreme Court's long-established Free Speech jurisprudence when passing judgment on articles of impeachment.

The Constitution must, at a minimum, serve as a limitation on the ability of Congress to impeach for "high crimes and misdemeanors." As noted by a Constitutional scholar a few years ago, if that were not the case, there would be a host of internal contradictions within the Constitution that could not have been intended by the Framers:

> Additional *negative* restrictions would also extend from the panoply of protections in the Bill of Rights. For example, an officer could not be removed from office for refusing to self-incriminate (Fifth Amendment) or seeking the assistance of counsel in a criminal prosecution (Sixth Amendment). Whatever "high crimes and Misdemeanors" means, it cannot include conduct that is itself protected by the Constitution; such would be an internal contradiction. Or, to frame it in modern doctrine, it would amount

---

98 While the First Amendment explicitly states that "Congress shall make no laws" abridging freedom of speech or of the press, by settled tradition it "has been read to apply to the entire national government." U.S. Constitution, 1st Am.; Gerald Gunther, *Constitutional Law, Cases and Materials* 462 (10th ed. 1982); *Valley Forge Christian Coll. v. Americans United for Separation of Church & State, Inc.*, 454 U.S. 464, 511 (1982) (Brennan, J. dissenting on other grounds) ("The First Amendment binds the Government as a whole, regardless of which branch is at work in a particular instance."); *Richmond Newspapers*, 448 U.S. at 575 ("The First Amendment . . . prohibits governments from 'abridging the freedom of speech, or of the press."); *Smith v. California*, 361 U.S. 147, 157 (1960) (Black, J., concurring) ("The First Amendment . . . fixed its own value on freedom of speech and press by putting these freedoms wholly 'beyond the reach' of federal power to abridge.").

99 U.S. Senate Website, *Oath of Office,* https://www.senate.gov/artandhistory/history/common/briefing/Oath_Office.htm

> to an unconstitutional condition: punishing a person for exercising a right protected by the Constitution.[100]

The position advanced by the House Managers is essentially an impeachment standard without Constitutional guardrails, unmoored to any specific legal test other than the unbridled whims of the House Managers. That distinctly was not what the Framers intended when they expressly limited impeachable offenses to "high crimes and misdemeanors." The Framers of the Constitution were keenly aware of the danger of any impeachment process that would make the President "the mere creature of the Legislature."[101] Such an arrangement would constitute nothing less than "a violation of the fundamental principle of good Government."[102]

Founding Father James Wilson, who was a renowned legal scholar, served as one of the six initial Supreme Court Justices (1789-1798), and was a major force in drafting the Constitution,[103] plainly stated in his law lectures that lawful and constitutional conduct may not be used as an impeachable offense:

> The doctrine of impeachments is of high import in the constitutions of free states. On one hand, the most powerful magistrates should be amenable to the law: on the other hand, elevated characters should not be sacrificed merely on account of their elevation. No

---

100 Josh Blackman, *Obstruction of Justice and the Presidency: Part II*, Lawfare (Dec. 12, 2017)(emphasis original), https://www.lawfareblog.com/obstruction-justice-and-presidency-part-i.

101 2 *Records of the Federal Convention of 1787*, at 86 (Max Farrand ed., rev. ed. 1937).

102 *Id.*

103 "James Wilson (September 14, 1742 – August 21, 1798) was an American statesmen, politician, legal scholar, and Founding Father who served as an Associate Justice of the United States Supreme Court from 1789 to 1798. He was elected twice to the Continental Congress, was a signatory of the United States Declaration of Independence, and was a major force in drafting the United States Constitution. A leading legal theorist, he was one of the six original justices appointed by George Washington to the Supreme Court of the United States. In his capacity as first Professor of Law at the University of Pennsylvania, he taught the first course on the new Constitution to President Washington and his cabinet in 1789 and 1790." https://en.wikipedia.org/wiki/James_Wilson_(founding_father)

> one should be secure while he violates the constitution and the laws: ***everyone should be secure while he observes them***.[104]

The House Managers' suggestion that the First Amendment does not apply to this impeachment process is untenable. It conflicts with common sense, the Senators' Oath of Office, well-settled Supreme Court precedent, and the intent of the Framers of the Constitution, such as James Wilson, who not only was a draftsman of the Constitution, but taught the first course on the new Constitution to President Washington and his cabinet in Philadelphia at the University of Pennsylvania in 1789. The Senate should soundly reject the Managers' invitation to disregard the Constitution.

2. Mr. Trump as an Elected Official Has First Amendment Rights to Freely Engage in Political Speech

Another roadblock the House Managers use is the legally unsupported idea that because Mr. Trump was an elected official, specifically the President, he has fewer rights under the First Amendment than everyone else in the United States. This, too, is sophistry. The opposite is true. The Supreme Court of the United States has long held that the First Amendment's right to freedom of speech protects elected officials such as Mr. Trump. The House Managers' argument to the contrary both ignores well-established precedent and erodes the constitutional principles guiding this august body. In fact, the argument of the House Managers so materially omits the relevant constitutional precepts that an extended discussion becomes both necessary and warranted, particularly in light of the public commentary relied upon in the House Trial Memorandum.

There can be no dispute that elected public officials engage in protected free speech when they speak out on investigations of voting regularity and fairness. The Supreme Court held that an elected sheriff who spoke out on an investigation of voting patterns, and even communicated

---

[104] *Collected Works of James Wilson*, Vol. 2 at 861 (Hall Kermit ed., 2007).

with a sitting grand jury via open letter, was protected by the First Amendment from punitive action by another group of "elected officers" for "publishing views honestly held and contrary to those" advocated by his accusers in the other political party.[105] Justice Brennan, writing for the majority in *Wood v. Georgia*, went so far as to make the protection of an elected public official a core First Amendment principle because the voting controversy at issue directly affected the sheriff's political career:

> The petitioner was an elected official and had the right to enter the field of political controversy, particularly where his political life was at stake. The role that elected officials play in our society makes it all the more imperative that they be allowed freely to express themselves on matters of current public importance.[106]

To paraphrase *Wood*, if Mr. Trump could be silenced in this manner by Congress, the Constitutional problem becomes evident: [107] a difference of political opinion, expressed in speech, on an issue of voting irregularity cannot be punishable where all that was done was to encourage investigation of voting irregularities and peaceful political speech.[108]

If *Wood* alone was not dispositive of Mr. Trump's free speech rights as an elected official to address public controversies such as voting irregularities and the authority of officials certifying votes, the Supreme Court emphatically held shortly after *Wood* that a legislature cannot punish an elected official for protected political speech. *Bond v. Floyd* squarely addresses the question of an

---

105 *Wood v. Georgia*, 370 U.S. 375, 390–91, 394-95 (1962).

106 *Wood*, 370 U.S. at 394-95 (citation and footnote omitted).

107 *Id.* at 390-91.

108 "I know that everyone here will soon be marching over to the Capitol building to peacefully and patriotically make your voices heard." Transcript of January 6, 2021 Speech at approximately 18:16, available at https://www.rev.com/blog/transcripts/donald-trump-speech-save-america-rally-transcript-january-6.

elected official's punishment by a legislature for statements alleged to have incited public violation of the law, unequivocally rejecting the idea that an elected official is entitled to lesser, or no, protection under the First Amendment. When the state argued "that even though such a citizen might be protected by his First Amendment rights, the State may nonetheless apply a stricter standard to its legislators[,]" the Supreme Court responded tersely, "We do not agree[,]" and held the action of the legislature against the elected official unconstitutional and in violation of his First Amendment rights.[109]

The *Bond* case is particularly instructive, because the petitioner opposed the Vietnam war draft, and was accused of endorsing the burning of draft cards—a position he subsequently clarified, noting that he possessed his own draft card and did not support burning draft cards.[110] As punishment for articulating this position in theoretical conflict with federal law, the Georgia House of Representatives to which he was elected refused to seat him—a purely legislative action, like impeachment.[111] Based in part upon Bond's subsequent clarification that he did not urge anyone to burn draft cards, the Supreme Court first concluded that Bond "could not have been constitutionally convicted under 50 U.S.C. App. s 462(a), which punishes any person who 'counsels, aids, or abets another to refuse or evade registration.'"[112]

Going further, the Supreme Court held that the Georgia House of Representatives was in fact forbidden by the First Amendment from punishing Bond for advocating against the policy of the United States. It began by once again rejecting outright the argument that an elected official

---

109 *Bond v. Floyd*, 385 U.S. 116, 132–33 (1966).

110 *Bond*, 385 U.S. at 118-25 ("I have not counselled burning draft cards, nor have I burned mine.")

111 *Id.* at 125.

112 *Id.* at 133-34.

could be held to any "higher standard" or that the Georgia House could "limit[] its legislators' capacity to discuss their views of local or national policy."[113] Justice Brennan, once again writing for the majority, went on to reaffirm the Constitutional shield around the speech of elected officials, even extending it to statements deemed "erroneous:"

> The manifest function of the First Amendment in a representative government requires that legislators be given the widest latitude to express their views on issues of policy. The central commitment of the First Amendment, as summarized in the opinion of the Court in *New York Times v. Sullivan*, 376 U.S. 254, 270, 84 S.Ct. 710, 721, 11 L.Ed.2d 686 (1964), is that 'debate on public issues should be uninhibited, robust, and wide-open.' We think the rationale of the *New York Times* case disposes of the claim that Bond's statements fell outside the range of constitutional protection. Just as erroneous statements must be protected to give freedom of expression the breathing space it needs to survive, so statements criticizing public policy and the implementation of it must be similarly protected. The State argues that the *New York Times* principle should not be extended to statements by a legislator because the policy of encouraging free debate about governmental operations only applies to the citizen-critic of his government. We find no support for this distinction in the *New York Times* case or in any other decision of this Court. The interest of the public in hearing all sides of a public issue is hardly advanced by extending more protection to citizen-critics than to legislators. Legislators have an obligation to take positions on controversial political questions so that their constituents can be fully informed by them, and be better able to assess their qualifications for office; also so they may be represented in governmental debates by the person they have elected to represent them.[114]

Mr. Trump's statements and advocacy of his political opinions—abhorred by the opponents of freedom of speech in the House as they may be—is no less protected than Bond's speech. Mr. Trump, having been elected nationally, was elected to be the voice for his national

---

[113] *Id.* at 135.

[114] *Id.* at 135-37.

constituency. It is undeniable that the First Amendment's protections flow to him as an elected official where he was, as Wood, addressing the electoral integrity issues essential to his career that he has consistently advocated, a position unpopular with his political opponents. Furthermore, as Mr. Trump expressly urged rally participants "to peacefully and patriotically make your voices heard"[115] on January 6, 2021, his political speech falls squarely within the protections of the First Amendment under clear Supreme Court precedent (as fully discussed below), and he thus cannot be convicted by a Senate sworn to uphold the Constitution.

Contrary to these express holdings of the Supreme Court, as announced more than fifty years ago, the House Managers assert in their memorandum that "the First Amendment does not shield public officials who occupy sensitive policymaking positions from adverse actions when their speech undermines important government interests."[116] In making this spurious claim, the Managers rely on two cases concerning *appointed* public employees,[117] having inexplicably failed to bring to the Senate's attention the squarely and obviously on-point Supreme Court authority concerning *elected* public officials (discussed at length *supra*).

The House Manager's two cases, however, address the wholly different situation of public defenders and sheriff's office employees suffering unconstitutional dismissals based on party affiliation. Those individuals were protected from employment termination—not impeachment—because they were not policy-makers or possessors of confidential information, and thus, their

115 Transcript of January 6, 2021 Speech at approximately 18:16, available at https://www.rev.com/blog/transcripts/donald-trump-speech-save-america-rally-transcript-january-6.

116 House Trial Memo. at 46.

117 *Branti v. Finkel*, 445 U.S. 507 (1980); *Elrod v. Burns*, 427 U.S. 347 (1976).

"private political beliefs" could not interfere with their duties.[118] Such cases cannot serve as the basis for a First Amendment analysis of Mr. Trump, or in fact any president, because elected officials are different in kind from non-elected public employees under the First Amendment.

The Supreme Court, in fact, expressly rejected the House Managers' First Amendment argument when confronting the voting investigation speech at issue in *Wood*.[119] Justice Brennan examined the line of cases addressing termination of non-elected public employees and found it inapplicable to the case of the elected sheriff:

> Petitioner was not a civil servant, but an elected official, and hence this is not a case like *United Public Workers v. Mitchell*, 330 U.S. 75, 67 S.Ct. 556, 91 L.Ed. 754, in which this Court held that congress has the power to circumscribe the political activities of federal employees in the career public service.

As *Mitchell* was the case relied upon in *Elrod*[120] and *Branti*,[121] and its factual predicate was expressly rejected as a basis for evaluation of an elected public official's First Amendment rights in *Wood*, the House Managers have built their case against the First Amendment upon the proverbial foundation of sand, and have no support for their argument that Mr. Trump lacks protection under the First Amendment as all Supreme Court authority is directly contrary to their assertions.

---

118 *Branti*, 445 U.S. at 517 (synthesizing rule in *Elrod*).

119 *Wood*, 370 U.S. at 395 n.21.

120 427 U.S. at 357, 362, 366-70.

121 445 U.S. at 515 n.10.

3. Mr. Trump's Speech Was Fully Protected by the First Amendment

Mr. Trump engaged in constitutionally protected political speech that the House has, improperly, characterized as "incitement of insurrection." The attempt of the House to transmute Mr. Trump's speech—core free speech under the First Amendment—into an impeachable offense cannot be supported, and convicting him would violate the very Constitution the Senate swears to uphold.

House Resolution 24 contains only one article of impeachment: incitement of insurrection.[122] The allegations made i that article are that Mr. Trump engaged in speech of various kinds concerning a public, political event: the Presidential election of November 2020. Specifically, House Resolution 24 focuses upon Mr. Trump's speech on January 6, 2021.[123] The article also discusses in passing other "statements" of Mr. Trump as well as a telephone call to the secretary of state of Georgia.[124]

The fatal flaw of the House's arguments is that it seeks to mete out governmental punishment – impeachment—based on political speech that falls squarely within broad protections of the First Amendment. Speech and association for political purposes is the kind of activity to which the First Amendment offers its strongest protection.[125] Restrictions placed on freedom of

---

122 H. Res. 24 at 2, 117th Cong. (Jan. 11, 2021). The sole article of impeachment is framed under the "high Crimes and Misdemeanors" clause of Article II, and does not allege treason or bribery. U.S. CONST. art. II, § 4.

123 *Id.* at 2-3.

124 *Id.* at 2, 4.

125 *New York Times Co. v.* Sullivan, 376 U.S. 254, 269 (1964)(The First Amendment "'was fashioned to assure unfettered interchange of ideas for the bringing about of political and social changes desired by the people.'" (quoting *Roth v. United States,* 354 U.S. 476, 484 (1957)).

speech are evaluated "against the background of a profound national commitment to the principle that debate on public issues should be uninhibited, robust, and wide open, and that it may well include vehement, caustic, and sometimes unpleasantly sharp attacks on government and public officials."[126] Thus, "[o]ur First Amendment decisions have created a rough hierarchy in the constitutional protection of speech" in which "[c]ore political speech occupies the highest, most protected position."[127]

The Supreme Court has further acknowledged that "[t]he language of the political arena . . . is often vituperative, abusive, and inexact."[128] A rule of law permitting criminal or civil liability to be imposed upon those who speak or write on public issues and their superintendence would lead to "self-censorship" by all which would not be relieved by permitting a defense of truth. "Under such a rule, would-be critics of official conduct may be deterred from voicing their criticism, even though it is believed to be true and even though it is in fact true, because of doubt whether it can be proved in court or fear of the expense of having to do so . . . . The rule thus dampens the vigor and limits the variety of public debate."[129] In only a few well defined and

---

126 *Watts v. United States*, 394 U.S. 705, 708 (1969) (quoting *New York Times Co. v. Sullivan*, 376 U.S. 254, 270 (1964)).

127 *R.A.V. v. St. Paul*, 505 U.S. 377, 422 (1992(Stevens, J., concurring); *see also Hill v. Colorado*, 530 U.S. 703, 787 (2000)(Kennedy, J., dissenting)("Laws punishing speech which protests the lawfulness or morality of the government's own policy are the essence of the tyrannical power the First Amendment guards against."); *Citizens United v. Federal Election Comm'n*, 588 U.S. 310, 349 (2010)("If the First Amendment has any force, it prohibits Congress from fining or jailing citizens, or associations of citizens, for simply engaging in political speech.")

128 *Watts*, 394 U.S. at 708 (distinguishing between "political hyperbole" and "true threats") (citing *Linn v. United Plant Guard Workers of America*, 383 U.S. 53, 58, (1966)).

129 *New York Times,* 376 U.S. at 279.

narrowly limited classes of speech may the government punish an individual for his or her words.[130]

Even political speech that *may* incite unlawful conduct is protected from the reach of governmental punishment. Indeed, "[e]very idea is an incitement,' and if speech may be suppressed whenever it *might* inspire someone to act unlawfully, then there is no limit to the State's censorial power."[131] The government may not prohibit speech because it increases the chance an unlawful act will be committed "at some indefinite future time."[132] Rather, the government may *only* suppress speech for advocating the use of force or a violation of law if **"such advocacy is directed to inciting or producing imminent lawless action and is likely to incite or produce such action."[133]**

In *Brandenburg v. Ohio*, the Supreme Court formed a test that placed even speech inciting illegal conduct within the protection of the First Amendment.[134] In that case, a leader of the Ku Klux Klan was convicted under an Ohio criminal syndicalism law.[135] Evidence of his incitement was a film of the events at a Klan rally, which included racist and anti-Semitic speech, the burning of a large wooden cross, and several items that appeared in the film, including a number of

---

130 *Gooding v. Wilson*, 405 U.S. 518, 521-22 (1972).

131 *Lorillard Tobacco Co. v. Reilly*, 533 U.S. 525, 580, 121 S.Ct. 2404, 2435, 150 L.Ed.2d 532 (2001)(emphasis added)(quoting *Gitlow v. New York*, 268 U.S. 652, 673, 45 S.Ct. 625, 69 L.Ed. 1138 (1925)(Holmes, J., dissenting)).

132 *Ashcroft v. Free Speech Coal.*, 535 U.S. 234, 253–54 (2002)(quoting *Hess v. Indiana*, 414 U.S. 105, 108 (1973)(*per curiam*)).

133 *Brandenburg v. Ohio*, 395 U.S. 444, 447 (1969) (emphasis added) (*per curiam*).

134 395 U.S. at 447.

135 *Id.* at 445.

firearms.[136] The leader of the protest proclaimed that "[w]e're not a revengent [sic] organization, but if our President, our Congress, our Supreme Court, continues to suppress the white, Caucasian race, it's possible that there might be some revenge taken. We are marching on Congress July the Fourth, four hundred thousand strong."[137] The Court held that, "the constitutional guarantees of free speech and free press do not permit [the government] to forbid or proscribe advocacy of the use of force or of law violation except where such advocacy is directed to inciting or producing imminent lawless action and is likely to incite or produce such action."[138] The Court explained that "the mere abstract teaching of the moral propriety or even moral necessity for a resort to force and violence, is not the same as preparing a group for violent action and steeling it to such action.[139]

Thus, under *Brandenburg* and its progeny, government actors may not "forbid or proscribe advocacy of the use of force or of law violation except where such advocacy is directed to inciting or producing imminent lawless action and is likely to incite or produce such action."[140] Absent an imminent threat, therefore, it is expressly within the First Amendment to advocate for the use of force; similarly, it is protected speech to advocate for violating the law; and as Mr. Trump did neither of these things, his speech at all times fell well within First Amendment protections. He thus cannot be subject to conviction by the Senate under well-established First Amendment jurisprudence.

---

136 *Id.* at 445-46.

137 *Id.* at 446.

138 *Id.*

139 *Id.* at 448.

140 *Id.*

The article of impeachment cherry picks Mr. Trump's phrases from an hour-long speech, and indeed other speeches before other audiences, but even looked at through the lens of House Resolution 24, the incitement alleged is sterile and thin. The House's case for "incitement" simply fails to pass constitutional muster.

First, Mr. Trump unambiguously advocated to the crowd at the January 6, 2021 event that he expected peaceful behavior. He explicitly stated, "I know that everyone here will soon be marching over to the Capitol building to ***peacefully*** and patriotically make your voices heard."[141] Indeed, after reports of violence at the Capitol Mr. Trump issued a public video statement, urging the crowd at the Capitol to "go home" in "peace" and further pleading:

> we have to have peace, we have to have law and order, we have to respect our great people in law and order, we don't want anyone hurt. . .[142]

Mr. Trump's explicit disavowal of violence and calls for peace – both directly before and after the riot – and his urge to have the participants use their "voices" as opposed to other action cannot be ignored. Given these express statements, and the fact that the First Amendment protects elected public officials who disclaim violence or violations of the law,[143] the inquiry need go no further. Mr. Trump incited no insurrection, and his speech as a whole (despite all of the rhetoric

---

141 Transcript of January 6, 2021 Speech at approximately 18:16 (emphasis added), available at https://www.rev.com/blog/transcripts/donald-trump-speech-save-america-rally-transcript-january-6.

142 Video Starting at :22, located at https://www.c-span.org/video/?507774-1/president-trump-claims-election-stolen-tells-protesters-leave-capitol.

143 *Bond*, 385 U.S. at 125, 133-34 ("I have not counselled burning draft cards, nor have I burned mine.").

in House Resolution 24) cannot support a conviction because the First Amendment protected him at all times from government retribution.

Second, the House's heavy reliance on Mr. Trump's metaphorical "fighting" language is completely devoid of context, which, when considered as a whole, places Mr. Trump's speech entirely within the protection of the First Amendment. The thrust of the House's allegation against Mr. Trump is that he said, in the context of election security generally, that "if you don't ***fight*** like hell you're not going to have a country anymore."[144] To characterize this statement alone as "incitement to insurrection" is to ignore, wholesale, the remainder of Mr. Trump's speech that day, including his call for his supporters to "peacefully" making their "voices heard."

What is more, a closer examination of the text of Mr. Trump's speech reveals he makes references to "fighting" in a plainly figurative sense. For example, the metaphor of boxing permeated Mr. Trump's speech. He expressly referred to the sport in his speech, associating it with the word "fighting:" "Republicans are constantly ***fighting*** like a boxer with his hands tied behind his back. It's like a boxer[.]"[145] The House cannot seriously argue that Mr. Trump's use of the word "fighting" in this speech incited an insurrection, given this usage; it is not merely couched in the language of simile ("like") but it describes a position of physical disadvantage; it is far from a prescription for future violent action.

Mr. Trump used the word "fights" in the figurative sense of arguing, or putting forth an extreme effort, just as he did a short time later, speaking of Rep. Jordan:

---

144 H. Res. 24 at 3, 117th Cong. (Jan. 11, 2021).

145 Transcript of January 6, 2021 Speech at approximately 16:25 (emphasis added).

> There's so many weak Republicans. We have great ones, Jim Jordan, and some of these guys. They're out there ***fighting*** the House. Guys are ***fighting***, but it's incredible.[146]

Mr. Trump again used the word "fighting," but Rep. Jordan was not punching any of his fellow representatives. Mr. Trump referred to Rep. Jordan's *advocacy* efforts. This is entirely consistent with yet another use of the word, in reference to action at the ballot box, not violence:

> Unbelievable, what we have to go through, what we have to go through and you have to get your people to ***fight***. If they don't ***fight***, we have to primary the hell out of the ones that don't ***fight***. You primary them. We're going to let you know who they are. I can already tell you, frankly.[147]

Again, Mr. Trump used the word "fight" in the sense of forceful argument, and combined it with a plainly nonviolent request: he sought a change in the occupants of Congress through future primary elections, not through violence.

None of this constituted anything from which a conviction may follow: Mr. Trump's speech on January 6, 2021 was protected political speech, that which receives the strongest protection under the First Amendment, when the protections of free speech are at their highest.[148] In fact, under *Brandenburg*, there is no doubt that the words upon which the article of impeachment issued could never support a conviction, as there was plainly no advocacy of "lawless action" and the words, as stated, can hardly be interpreted to be "likely" to "incite imminent" violence or lawless action.

---

146 *Id.* at approximately 12:34 (emphasis added).

147 *Id.* at approximately 13:45 (emphasis added).

148 *Arizona Free Enter. Club's Freedom Club PAC v. Bennett*, 564 U.S. 721, 734 (2011).

Neither can the other allegations in the article of impeachment support a conviction given Mr. Trump's plain and clear First Amendment protection. The allegations of other "statements" alleged to contribute to an "incitement of insurrection"[149] are bereft of detail, and even as expanded upon in the House Managers' Trial Memorandum, amount to no more than Mr. Trump's advocating his position that he won the Presidential election in November 2020.

The allegation that Mr. Trump should be convicted for "incitement of insurrection" based upon the telephone call to the Georgia secretary of state rests on even shakier ground. The allegations of "threats of death and violence" come not from Mr. Trump at all; they come from other individuals from the internet, not identified (nor identifiable) in the House Trial Memorandum, who took it upon themselves to make inane internet threats, which were not urged or "incited" by Mr. Trump in any way shape or form.[150] Examining the discussion with the Georgia secretary of state under the standard of "incitement," leads to the same conclusion as the January 6, 2021 statements of Mr. Trump: there is nothing said by Mr. Trump that urges "use of force" or "law violation" directed to producing imminent lawless action.[151]

Even the House Managers' sinister and selective summary of Mr. Trumps' call cannot meet the standard for "incitement:" the analysis of the Supreme Court in *Hess v. Indiana* makes this apparent.[152] The question is not, as the House Managers seek to frame it, whether Mr. Trump's call offends the House's sensibilities; it is whether the call—which is plainly political speech in

---

149 H. Res. 24 at 3, 117th Cong. (Jan. 11, 2021).

150 House Trial Memo. at 9-10.

151 *Brandenburg*, 395 U.S. at 447.

152 414 U.S. 105, 107-10 (1973).

the sense that *Woods* concerns political speech, no different than the sheriff's letter to the grand jurors[153]—is outside the First Amendment based on the limited classes of speech beyond its ambit.[154] Mr. Trump's call was not obscene, nor did it contain fighting words, nor incitement: it was a political call, and such political speech must receive the highest protection afforded under the First Amendment.

The events of January 6, 2021, at the Capitol were terrible. The loss of life of any citizen, let alone a member of the Capitol Police, is a tragedy, but impeaching a former President is not the answer. The Senate should vote to clear Mr. Trump of any wrongdoing: "the hostile reaction of a crowd does not transform protected speech into incitement."[155] What matters is the objective meaning of the words. Courts do not deem speech unprotected based on how it could possibly be contorted or misunderstood by an unreasonable listener. Rather, they engage in an objective inquiry to determine how a reasonable person would understand the words. Otherwise, speakers at public events would be put at the mercy of the unhinged reactions of their most unreasonable audience members. That is exactly what happened on January 6th, but the Senate, composed of reasonable and erudite members, can take a few minutes and read the speech themselves.

In *Brandenburg*, the Supreme Court erected an extremely high bar to proving incitement.[156] That test requires proof that "(1) the speech explicitly or implicitly encouraged the use of violence or lawless action, (2) the speaker intends that his speech will result in the use of violence or lawless

---

153 *Wood*, 370 U.S. at 390–91, 394-95.

154 *Hess*, 414 U.S. at 107-08.

155 *Bible Believers v. Wayne Co.*, 805 F.3d 228, 246 (6th Cir. 2015).

156 *James v. Meow Media, Inc.*, 300 F.3d 683, 698 (6th Cir. 2002) (en banc).

action, and (3) the imminent use of violence or lawless action is the likely result of his speech."[157] The allegations against Mr. Trump unquestionably fail as a matter of law because "[a]dvocacy for the use of force or lawless behavior, intent, and imminence, are all absent." [158]Thus, "[t]he doctrine of incitement has absolutely no application" to this case. [159]

First, as evident from the transcript and the video of the speech in question, Mr. Trump's statements did not advocate—or even mention—the use of any force whatsoever. Because "[t]he mere tendency of speech to encourage unlawful acts is not a sufficient reason for banning it,"[160] it is all the more true that a statement that "fails to specifically advocate" for the crowd "to take 'any action' cannot constitute incitement."[161] Indeed, Mr. Trump expressly made a specific demand in his speech that all members of the audience - all protestors - behave "peacefully."

As the Sixth Circuit has recognized, "[i]t is not an easy task to find that speech rises to such a dangerous level that it can be deemed incitement to riot."[162] And unsurprisingly, "[t]here will rarely be enough evidence to create a jury question on whether a speaker was intending to incite imminent crime."[163] Consider *Hess v. Indiana*, where a protester yelled, "We'll take the fucking street again," to a crowd that was already agitated and resisting police.[164] The Court held

---

157 *Bible Believers v. Wayne Cty., Mich.*, 805 F.3d 228, 246 (6th Cir. 2015).

158 *Id.* at 244.

159 *Id.*

160 *Ashcroft v. Free Speech Coal.*, 535 U.S. 234, 253 (2002).

161 *Bible Believers*, 805 F.3d at 244 (quoting *Hess v. Indiana,* 414 U.S. 105, 109 (1973)).

162 *Id.*

163 Eugene Volokh, *Crime–Facilitating Speech*, 57 STAN. L. REV. 1095, 1190 (2005).

164 414 U.S. at 107.

that speech could not be punished.[165] Or take *NAACP v. Claiborne Hardware Co.*, where a speaker told a crowd that anyone who failed to boycott businesses would be "disciplined," and said, "If we catch any of you going in any of them racist stores, we're gonna break your damn neck."[166] The Court held that this speech was not incitement.[167] If these incendiary statements, with express references to violence, do not rise to the level of incitement, then surely Mr. Trump's request to peacefully protest could never be incitement.

In *Bible Believers*, the Court held the speech did not amount to incitement to riot under the *Brandenburg* test, despite the obviously explosive context, because it did not include "a single word" that could be perceived as encouraging, explicitly or implicitly, violence or lawlessness.[168] The same can be said of Mr. Trump's speech in this case: not a single word encouraged violence or lawlessness, explicitly or implicitly, and again, he affirmatively exhorted the crowd to act "peacefully" when protesting. Moreover, the *Bible Believers* court observed that "[t]he hostile reaction of a crowd does not transform protected speech into incitement."[169] Even though the Bible Believers' speech actually triggered a predictably violent reaction, it was their speech that the court scrutinized. And their speech was held to be protected, despite its blatantly offensive and even provocative nature and despite the crowd's reaction. It follows that if Mr. Trump's speech is protected—because it, like that of the Bible Believers, did not include a single word encouraging violence—then the fact that audience members reacted by using force does not transform Mr.

---

165 *Id.*

166 *NAACP v. Claiborne Hardware Co*, 458 U.S. 886, 902 (1982).

167 *Id.* at 928–29.

168 *Id.* at 246.

169 *Id.*

Trump's protected speech into unprotected speech. The reaction of listeners who may or may not be hostile does not alter the otherwise protected nature of speech.[170]

Nor is "the mere tendency of speech to encourage unlawful acts ... sufficient reason for banning it."[171] What is required, to forfeit constitutional protection, is incitement speech that "specifically advocate[s]" for listeners to take unlawful action.[172] Again, even assuming that then-President Trump's words may arguably have had a tendency to encourage unlawful use of force (which they did not), they certainly did not specifically advocate for listeners to take unlawful action and are therefore protected. As the *Bible Believers* court further observed, "[i]t is not an easy task to find that speech rises to such a dangerous level that it can be deemed incitement to riot."[173] The words alleged in the current case, much less offensive than those of the Bible Believers, are not up to the high standard demanded by *Brandenburg*.

Because not a single word of the speech actually advocates violence either implicitly or explicitly, the first *Brandenburg* factor—specific advocacy of violence— is totally absent. The allegations in the Article seems to place heavy reliance on the latter two *Brandenburg* factors. That is, the allegations that Mr. Trump intended violence to occur and knew that his words were likely to result in violence. But this backwards approach was specifically rejected in *Hess v. Indiana*, where the Court reversed the judgment of the Indiana Supreme Court.[174] In *Hess*, the Court noted that the state court had placed primary reliance on evidence that the speaker's

---

170 *Forsyth County, Georgia v. Nationalist Movement*, 505 U.S. 123 (1992).

171 *Ashcroft v. Free Speech Coal.*, 535 U.S. 234, 253, 122 S.Ct. 1389, 152 L.Ed.2d 403 (2002).

172 *Id.* (citing *Hess*, 414 U.S. at 109.

173 *Id.* at 244.

174 *Hess v. Indiana* 414 U.S. at 107–09.

statement was intended to incite further lawless action and was likely to produce such action. This was not enough. The *Hess* Court focused on the words, on the language, that comprised the subject speech, i.e., the first *Brandenburg* factor. "It hardly needs repeating," the Court repeated, "that the constitutional guarantees of freedom of speech forbid the States to punish the use of words or language not within narrowly limited classes of speech."[175] And in applying this wisdom, the Court likewise tied its conclusion to the words of the subject speech: "And since there was no evidence or rational inference from the import of the language, that his words were intended to produce, and likely to produce, imminent disorder, those words could not be punished by the State on the ground that they had 'a tendency to lead to violence.'"[176]

In other words, *Hess* teaches that the speaker's intent to encourage violence (second factor) and the tendency of his statement to result in violence (third factor) are not enough to forfeit First Amendment protection unless the words used specifically advocated the use of violence, whether explicitly or implicitly (first factor).

In *Snyder v. Phelps*, the Court observed: "[T]he court is obligated to make an independent examination of the whole record in order to make sure that the judgment does not constitute a forbidden intrusion on the field of free expression. In considering content, form, and context, no factor is dispositive, and it is necessary to evaluate all the circumstances of the speech, including what was said, where it was said, and how it was said."[177] So, yes, in addition to the content and form of the words, the Senate is obliged to consider the context, based on the whole record. (But not instead of it.)

---

175 *Id.* at 107 (quoting Gooding v. Wilson, 405 U.S. 518, 521–22 (1972)) (internal quotation marks omitted; emphasis added).

176 *Id.* at 109 (quoting the Indiana court's rationale) (emphasis added).

177 *Snyder v. Phelps*, 562 U.S. 443, 453 – 54 (2011) (internal quotation marks and citations omitted).

Here, of course, the "whole record" consists of the charges in the Article. An article of impeachment is literally a "charge" of particular wrongdoing. Thus, under the division of responsibility in the Constitution, the Senate must conduct a trial solely on the charge specified in articles of impeachment approved by a vote of the House and presented to the Senate. The Senate cannot expand the scope of a trial to consider mere assertions appearing in biased media reports that the House did not include in the articles of impeachment submitted to a vote of that Chamber, nor even in the unsupported statements in the House Managers' Trial Memorandum. Similarly, House Managers trying the case in the Senate must be confined to the specific conduct alleged in the Articles approved by the House. These restrictions follow both from the plain terms of the Constitution limiting the Senate to trying an "impeachment" framed by the House and from elementary principles of due process. "[T]he senator's role is solely one of acting on the accusations (Articles of Impeachment) voted by the House of Representatives. The Senate cannot lawfully find the president guilty of something not charged by the House, any more than a trial jury can find a defendant guilty of something not charged in the indictment." "No principle of procedural due process is more clearly established than that notice of the specific charge, and a chance to be heard in a trial of the issues raised by that charge, if desired, are among the constitutional rights of every accused."[178]

As the Supreme Court has explained, it has been the rule for over 130 years that "a court cannot permit a defendant to be tried on charges that are not made in the indictment against him."[179]

---

178 *Cole v. Arkansas*, 333 U.S. 196, 201 (1948).

179 *Stirone v. United States*, 361 U.S. 212, 217 (1960).

Doing so is "fatal error."[180] Under the same principles of due process, the Senate must similarly refuse to consider any uncharged allegations as a basis for conviction.

In its examination of context, the *Snyder* Court held that because the speech was protected, its setting, or context, could not render it unprotected.[181] In fact, Mr. Trump's admonition not to harm is analogous to the circumstance considered in *Bible Believers* as neutralizing the inciting tendency of words that were even more offensive in nature and delivered in an even more volatile context.

Even taking every one of Mr. Trump's prior statements about the election in the most negative light, they were, at most, only abstract discussions that never advocated for physical force. And even if they had broached the idea of violence, "the mere abstract teaching … of the moral propriety or even moral necessity for a resort to force and violence, is not the same as preparing a group for violent action and steeling it to such action."[182] Indeed there had never been violence before and so there was thus no reason to expect that Mr. Trump's statements would lead to any injury to the officers or protesters. Moreover, even, assuming *arguendo*, if one could posit that the likely response to that statement would have been "imminent lawless action,"[183] Mr. Trump corrected any such misunderstanding by immediately saying "Stay Peaceful!"

The fact that some small percentage of unlawful rioters who, as the FBI already knew in advance, had been planning to come and wage war, did so later that same day, does not in any way mean that they were acting at Mr. Trump's direction or through any "incitement" from Mr. Trump.

---

180 *Id.*

181 *Snyder*, 562 U.S. at 454–55.

182 *Noto v. United States*, 367 U.S. 290, 298 (1961).

183 *Brandenburg*, 395 U.S. at 447.

In the context of ordinary civil litigation, such a "bald" allegation of agency "is by itself a mere legal conclusion and is therefore insufficient to withstand a motion to dismiss."[184] "A complaint relying on agency must plead facts which, if proved, could establish the existence of an agency relationship. It is insufficient to merely plead the legal conclusion of agency."[185] "Neither a single incident nor sporadic incidents are sufficient to establish foreseeability."[186]

For First Amendment purposes, the meaning of words must be judged objectively. Unprotected speech is the exception to the rule of free speech, so it cannot be punished on the ground that it might be unprotected. The speech must objectively fall within the narrow exception for unprotected speech, lest protected speech be penalized based on a subjective or idiosyncratic interpretation.[187] Courts "weigh the circumstances in order to protect, not to destroy, freedom of speech."[188] "[I]f the freedoms of expression are to have the breathing space that they need to survive,"[189] courts must "err on the side of protecting political speech."[190] Here, the question is not even close. Mr. Trump's words are core speech protected under the First Amendment.

---

184 *Prochaska & Associates, Inc. v. Merrill Lynch Pierce Fenner & Smith, Inc.*, 798 F.Supp. 1427, 1433 (D. Neb. 1992).

185 *Bird v. Delacruz*, 2005 WL 1625303, at *4 (S.D. Ohio July 6, 2005); *see also Nuevo Mundo Holdings v. PriceWaterhouseCoopers LLP*, 2004 WL 112948, at *6 (S.D.N.Y. 2004).

186 *Grisham v. Wal-Mart Stores, Inc.*, 929 F.Supp. 1054, 1058 (E.D. Ky. 1995), aff'd sub nom., 89 F.3d 833 (6th Cir. 1996).

187 *See Claiborne*, 458 U.S. at 915 n.50.

188 *Cox v. Louisiana*, 379 U.S. 536, 578 (1965) (Black, J, concurring); *Bible Believers*, 805 F.3d at 234 ("We interpret the First Amendment broadly so as to favor allowing more speech.").

189 *New York Times Co.* ,376 U.S. at 271-72.

190 *FEC v. Wisconsin Right to Life, Inc.*, 551 U.S. 449, 457 (2007).

4. Lastly, Mr. Trump's Figurative Use of the Words "Fight," "Fighting," Have Been Used By Many, None Are Impeachable

It is truly incredible that House Democratic leadership is feigning horror at the President's choices of words considering some of their own members recent public comments. For example, in 2018, Speaker Nancy Pelosi held her weekly press conference in the Capitol Visitor Center. In reference to a policy she disagreed with, the most powerful Democrat in the Country said: "I just don't even know why there aren't uprisings all over the country. Maybe there will be."[191] Was she advocating violence? Sending a silent dog whistle to radical protesters? Should she be held accountable for her extremist rhetoric and removed from office?

As political violence grew last summer, Representative Ayana Pressley went on national TV and said that "there needs to be unrest in the streets." Should we hold her liable to pay for all of the businesses that were destroyed when people heeded her call and removed from office ?[192]

In perhaps the most egregious call for physical confrontation, Rep Maxine Waters told a crowd at a rally that they should accost members of the government that they do not like.

> You think we're rallying now? You ain't seen nothing yet...Already you have members of your Cabinet that are being booed out of restaurants ... protesters taking up at their house saying 'no peace, no sleep...If you see anybody from that Cabinet in a restaurant, in a department store, at a gasoline station, you get out and you create a crowd and you push back on them and you tell them they're not welcome anymore, anywhere... We want history to record that we stood up, that we pushed back, that we fought...

---

[191] Douglas Ernst, *Nancy Pelosi wonders why there 'aren't uprisings' across nation: 'Maybe there will be,'* The Washington Times (Jun. 14, 2018), https://www.washingtontimes.com/news/2018/jun/14/nancy-pelosi-wonders-why-there-arent-uprisings-acr/

[192] Am Joy, *Post Office Cuts Are War Against American People Pressley Says*, MSNBC (Aug. 15, 2020), https://www.msnbc.com/am-joy/watch/post-office-cuts-are-war-against-american-people-pressley-says-90125893871

In another cable interview Waters was even more specific:

> I have no sympathy for these people that are in this administration … they won't be able to go to a restaurant, they won't be able to stop at a gas station, they're not going to be able to shop at a department store. The people are going to turn on them. They're going to protest. They're absolutely going to harass them…We've got to push back.

In that instance, even Speaker Pelosi called Representative Waters' remarks "unacceptable" but of course did nothing to remove her from office, just like she has done nothing to censure other Members who have tweeted calls for genocide[193] – because when it is her side of the aisle making their 'political speech' heard, Speaker Pelosi is nothing if not tolerant. Other Democratic leadership went so far as to defend Representative Waters by bending over backwards to read an inverted message of peacefulness into her violent statements – the *exact opposite* of what they did to former President Trump. Giving her far more than the benefit of the doubt, Representative Cedric Richmond claimed that "[i]n exercising her constitutional right to freedom of speech at a recent rally, Congresswoman Waters did not, as she has made clear, encourage violence . . . She instead, encouraged Americans to exercise their constitutional rights to freedom of speech and peaceful assembly…" For those who would say that those quotes must be understood in their greater context, *i.e.*, that they were clearly meant to be political speech- we say *exactly.* The truth is that both the Mr. Trump's speech and these comments are acceptable political free speech; it is the double standard at play here that is entirely unacceptable, and Mr. Trump ask that the Senate reject it in no uncertain terms.

---

193 Aaron Bandler, *Rashida Tlaib Retweets 'From the River to the Sea'Tweet,* Jewish Journal (Nov. 30, 2020), https://jewishjournal.com/news/325415/rashida-tlaib-retweets-from-the-river-to-the-sea-tweet/

This is not the first time that Congress has impeached and tried to convict a President for making a speech, and the last time did not work either. The tenth Article of Impeachment against Andrew Johnson read as follows:

> That said Andrew Johnson, President of the United States, unmindful of the high duties of his office and the dignity and proprieties thereof, and of the harmony and courtesies which ought to exist and be maintained between the executive and legislative branches of the government of the United States, designing and intending to set aside the rightful authority and powers of Congress, did attempt to bring into disgrace, ridicule, hatred, contempt and reproach the Congress of the United States, and the several branches thereof, to impair and destroy the regard and respect of all the good people of the United States for the Congress and legislative power thereof (which all officers of the government ought inviolably to preserve and maintain,) and to excite the odium and resentment of all the good people of the United States against Congress and the laws by it duly and constitutionally enacted; and in pursuance of his said design and intent, openly and publicly, and before divers assemblages of the citizens of the United States convened in divers parts thereof to meet and receive said Andrew Johnson as the Chief Magistrate of the United States, did, ... make and deliver with a loud voice certain intemperate, inflammatory[,] and scandalous harangues, and did therein utter loud threats and bitter menaces as well against Congress as the laws of the United States duly enacted thereby, amid the cries[,] jeers[,] and laughter of the multitudes ... Which said utterances, declarations, threats[,] and harangues, highly censurable in any, are peculiarly indecent and unbecoming in the Chief Magistrate of the United States[.

While no vote was ever taken on the tenth Article, multiple Senators expressed their concern about trying to impeach for inflammatory rhetoric. James Patterson noted that "in view of the liberty of speech which our laws authorize, in view of the culpable license of speech which is practiced and allowed in other branches of the Government, I doubt if we can at present make low and scurrilous speeches a ground of impeachment."[194] Senator Sherman echoed this view;

---

194 CONG. GLOBE, 40th Cong., 2d Sess. 509 (Supp. 1868); *see also* Shaw, *Impeachable Speech*, 70 Emory L.J. 1, 21.

while indicating his support for conviction on a number of the other articles, he voiced concerns about the tenth article, arguing that "we must guard against making crimes out of mere political differences or the abuse of the freedom of speech."[195]

D. The House Afforded President Trump No Due Process of Law

On January 12th, Speaker Pelosi announced the nine representatives who would serve as the impeachment managers. On January 13, 2021, mere days after the press conference purportedly launching the inquiry, House Democrats completed the fastest presidential impeachment inquiry in history and adopted the Article of Impeachment over strong opposition and with zero due process of law afforded to the President, against Constitutional requirements and centuries of practice. The lack of due process is no small matter; due process of law is not a formality it is a

---

195 *Impeachable Speech*, 70 Emory L.J. at 62:

> There have also been recent suggestions that the invocation of presidential speech in a trial setting raises First Amendment concerns. Judge Kozinski made this claim in an opinion regarding one of the challenges to President Trump's first "travel ban" executive order. *Washington v. Trump*, 858 F.3d 1168, 1173 (9th Cir. 2017) (Kozinski, J., dissenting). Dissenting from the denial of rehearing en banc, Judge Kozinski criticized the panel for citing "a trove of informal and unofficial statements from the President and his advisers." *Id.* This approach, Kozinski warned, threatened to "chill campaign speech, despite the fact that our most basic free speech principles have their 'fullest and most urgent application precisely to the conduct of campaigns for political office.'" *Id.* (citing *McCutcheon v. FEC*, 572 U.S. 185, 191-192 (2014)). Given the near-constant campaigning in which an incumbent president might engage, this argument could be extended to virtually every statement a president makes--including in the context of an impeachment inquiry.

See also Paul F. Campos, *A Constitution for the Age of Demagogues: Using the Twenty-Fifth Amendment to Remove an Unfit President*, 97 Denv. L. Rev. 85, 100 (2019), noting that "Impeachment, in practice, has become something intended solely to remove a corrupt president…"; and Bushnell, Eleanore. *Crimes, Follies, and Misfortunes: The Federal Impeachment Trials*. University of Illinois Press, 1992, p. 6, noting that "The impeachment procedure was designed to provide a means for removing a deficient officer, not to punish for derelictions of duty or substitute for a court trial. Therefore, it might seem obvious that no action need be taken when a suspect occupant removed himself from his position."

key Constitutional right, and when it is lacking a case is tainted and the case should be dismissed. In the civil context, the law is clear that a case should be dismissed if the government wrongfully interfered with a defendant's due process rights, and that "[a]t the core of procedural due process jurisprudence is the right to advance notice of significant deprivations of liberty or property and to a meaningful opportunity to be heard." *Abbott v. Latshaw*, 164 F.3d 141, 146 (3d Cir.1998).

As it relates to impeachment proceedings, the legal analog is clear:

> The gravity of the deprivation at stake in an impeachment—especially a presidential impeachment—buttresses the conclusion that some due process limitations must apply. It would be incompatible with the Framers' understanding of the "delicacy and magnitude of a trust which so deeply concerns the political reputation and existence of every man engaged in the administration of public affairs"[196] to think that they envisioned a system in which the House was free to devise any arbitrary or unfair mechanism it wished for impeaching individuals. The Supreme Court has described due process as "the protection of the individual against arbitrary action."[197] There is no reason to think that protection was not intended to extend to impeachments.[198]

And in terms of longstanding historical practice when it comes to those proceedings, the precedent is also unambiguous:

> Although constitutional requirements governing House impeachment proceedings may have been unsettled when the Constitution was adopted, by the 1870s consistent practice in the House (unbroken since then) gave meaning to the Constitution and settled the minimum procedures that must be afforded for a fair impeachment inquiry. The Framers, who debated impeachment with reference to the contemporaneous English impeachment of Warren

---

196 *The Federalist* No. 65, *supra* note at 397 (Alexander Hamilton).

197 *Ohio Bell Tel. Co. v. Pub. Serv. Comm'n,* 301 U.S. 292, 302 (1937).

198 Trial Memorandum of President Donald J. Trump (2020); *Hastings v. United States*, 802 F. Supp. 490, 504 (D.D.C. 1992), *vacated and remanded on other grounds by Hastings v. United States*, 988 F.2d 1280 (D.C. Cir. 1993) (per curiam).

> Hastings,[199] knew that "the House of Commons did hear the accused, and did permit him to produce testimony, before they voted an impeachment against him."[200] And practice in the United States rapidly established that the accused in an impeachment must be allowed fair process. Although a few early impeachment investigations were *ex parte*,[201] the House provided the accused with notice and an opportunity to be heard in the majority of cases starting as early as 1818.[202]

Democratic Members of the House have argued that then-President Trump's alleged offense was so grave and his power so immense that there was no time to wait for the actual facts to come to light. In a crocodile-tear-stained letter, Representative Ilhan Omar, herself no stranger to extremist rhetoric,[203] exhorted her colleagues by saying, "The urgency of this moment is real and we have to be courageous and unified in defense of our Republic...Every single hour that Donald Trump remains in office, our country, our democracy, and our national security remain in danger. Congress must take immediate action to keep the people of this country safe and set a precedent

---

199 2 *Records of the Federal Convention of 1787*, at 550 (M. Farrand ed. 1966); *see, e.g.*, Richard M. Pious, *Impeaching the President: The Intersection of Constitutional and Popular Law*, 43 St. Louis L.J. 859, 872 (1999); *see also, e.g.*, *Proceedings of the Senate Sitting for the Trial of William W. Belknap, Late Secretary of War, on the Articles of Impeachment Exhibited by the House of Representatives*, 44th Cong. 98 (1876) (statement of Sen. Timothy Howe); Scott S. Barker, *An Overview of Presidential Impeachment*, 47 Colo. Lawyer 30, 32 (Sept. 2018).

200 6 Reg. Deb. 737 (1830) (statement of Rep. James Buchanan).

201 *See* III Hinds' Precedents § 2319, at 681 (Judge Pickering); *id.* § 2343, at 716 (Justice Chase).

202 *See* 32 Annals of Cong. 1715, 1715–16 (1818); *see, e.g.*, III Hinds' Precedents § 2491, at 988 (Judge Thurston, 1825); *id.* § 1736, at 97–98 (Vice President Calhoun, 1826); *id.* §§ 2365–2366 (Judge Peck, 1830–1831); *id.* § 2491, at 989 (Judge Thurston, 1837); *id.* § 2495, at 994 & n.4 (Judge Watrous, 1852); Cong. Globe, 35th Cong., 1st Sess. 2167 (1858) (statement of Rep. Horace Clark) (Judge Watrous, 1858); III Hinds' Precedents § 2496, at 999 (Judge Watrous, 1858); *id.* § 2504, at 1008 (Judge Delahay, 1873).

203 Sarah Elbeshbishi, Nicholas Wu, *GOP targets Ihan Omar after Dems try to Oust Majorie Taylor Green,* USA Today (Feb. 4, 2021), https://www.usatoday.com/story/news/politics/2021/02/03/gop-targets-ilhan-omar-after-dems-try-oust-marjorie-taylor-green/4369715001/ and Rep Andy Biggs, Twitter (Feb. 3, 2021, 9:02 AM), https://twitter.com/RepAndyBiggsAZ/status/1356966391493111808.

that such behavior cannot be tolerated." Of course, President Trump's term came to an end without the apocalyptic predictions of the all-seeing Rep. Omar coming to pass.

As Speaker Pelosi told the country, she had to act *now* "so urgent was the matter." So urgent, of course, that instead of immediately sending it over to the Senate so that the President could have a trial and, if convicted, be removed, the Speaker once again decided to act in a purely political manner, pretending that she was rushing the impeachment to protect the country from an imminent danger, and then waiting until the President was no longer in the White House to prefer the charge. The House actually took longer t o transmit the Article of Impeachment to the Senate than it did to investigate and debate it in the first place.

Of course, this is not the first time that Speaker Pelosi has ignored the Constitutional protections in an impeachment proceeding. When they led the impeachment of then-President Trump the first time, the Democratic leadership also denied him due process (although not as brazenly and outrageously as this time) and the Speaker also refused to send the Articles of Impeachment to the Senate right away. That time, her machinations were focused on trying to influence the rules that the Senate would put in place for the trial, and she only sent the articles to the Senate when it became clear that she would not get her way. [204] But, just like this time, in withholding the articles the Speaker undercut one of her party's "primary arguments for impeachment in the first place: the need for urgency in removing Trump."[205] As Democratic

---

[204] John Hulsman, *In the impeachment saga trump derangement syndrome is destroying the Democrats*, City A.M. (Jan. 20, 2020), https://www.cityam.com/in-the-impeachment-saga-trump-derangement-syndrome-is-destroying-the-democrats/ ("Republican Senate majority leader Mitch McConnell, as shrewd a tactician as Pelosi herself, had the speaker's number, and he has been grimly clear in response to the issue of Pelosi trying to leverage him: "We will not cede our (Senate) authority to try this impeachment. The House Democrats' turn is over.")

[205] *Id.*

senator and staunch Pelosi ally Dianne Feinstein put it: "'The longer it goes on, the less urgent it becomes. So if it's serious and urgent, send them over. If it isn't, don't send it over.'"[206]

This time the Speaker apparently held the Articles over so that she could effectively, maneuver an ally in the Senate into the judge's chair. Once the 45th President's term expired, and the House chose to allow jurisdiction to lapse on the Article of Impeachment, the constitutional mandate for the Chief Justice to preside at all impeachments involving the President disappears. Now, instead of the Chief Justice, the trial will be overseen by a biased and partisan Senator who will purportedly *also act as a juror* while ruling on issues that arise during trial.

The Senate, in reviewing the House actions, should immediately dismiss this case because the process was completely unfair and one-sided. The civil analog is clear: "Every federal appellate court has a special obligation to 'satisfy itself not only of its own jurisdiction, but also that of the lower courts in a cause under review,' even though the parties are prepared to concede it."[207]

Throughout this entire process Speaker Pelosi was never acting to apply her understanding of the laws of impeachment in any principled manner. The Speaker did *not* think it was necessary to call for an impeachment so long as she got her way, and twice told the Vice President, and the country, just that. She did *not* really believe that the process was "urgent " and it was *never* actually about whether President Donald Trump would stay in office, because once she brought the impeachment Article to a vote she decided to hold it until after he had finished the remainder of his term. If the Speaker really believed that the President was that much of a danger, then she was being criminally negligent by holding it back. Obviously, as demonstrated by her actions, there

---

206 *Id.*

207 *Steel Co. v. Citizens for a Better Env't*, 523 U.S. 83, 95, 118 S. Ct. 1003, 1013 (1998) (interior quotation omitted).

was only ever one urgency, to score political points quickly before the harried Members of even her own party could calm down and look at the facts. And there was only ever one motivation; to try and spin this incredibly sad moment in American history, and use it to embarrass the President. Unfortunately for House Democrats, the impeachment of a former United States President, a private citizen, is unconstitutional.

E. The Article Is Structurally Deficient and Can Only Result in Acquittal.

The hastily drafted Article is not only wrong on the facts and the law, it also suffers from a Constitutionally fatal structural defect that the Senate cannot remedy. This defect alone makes it worthy of dismissal:

> Put simply, the articles are impermissibly duplicitous—that is, each article charges multiple different acts as possible grounds for sustaining a conviction.[208] The problem with an article offering such a menu of options is that the Constitution requires two-thirds of Senators present to agree ***on the specific basis for conviction***. A vote on a duplicitous article, however, could never provide certainty that a two-thirds majority had actually agreed upon a ground for conviction. Instead, such a vote could be the product of an amalgamation of votes resting on several different theories, no single one of which would have garnered two-thirds support if it had been presented separately. Accordingly, duplicitous articles like those exhibited here are facially unconstitutional.[209]

As noted in our previously filed Answer to the Charges, by charging multiple alleged wrongs in one article, the House of Representatives has made it impossible to guarantee compliance with the Constitutional mandate in Article 1, Sec. 3, Cl. 6 that permits a conviction only by at least two-thirds of the members. The House charge fails by interweaving differing allegations rather than

---

208 "'Duplicity' is the joining of two or more distinct and separate offenses in a single count"; "'[m]ultiplicity' is charging a single offense in several counts." 1A Charles Alan Wright et al., *Federal Practice and Procedure* § 142 (4th ed. 2019); *see, e.g.*, *United States v. Root*, 585 F.3d 145, 150 (3d Cir. 2009); *United States v. Chrane*, 529 F.2d 1236, 1237 n.3 (5th Cir. 1976).

209 House Trial Memo 2020.

breaking them out into counts of alleged individual instances of misconduct. Rule XXIII of the *Rules of Procedure and Practice in the Senate When Sitting on Impeachment Trials* provides, in pertinent part, that an article of impeachment shall not be divisible thereon. Because the Article at issue here alleges multiple wrongs in the single article, it would be impossible to know if two-thirds of the members agreed on the entire article, or just on parts, as the basis for vote to convict. The House failed to adhere to strict Senate rules and, instead, chose to make the Article as broad as possible intentionally in the hope that some Senators might agree with parts, and other Senators agree with other parts, but that when these groups of senators were added together, the House might achieve the appearance of two thirds in agreement, when those two thirds of members, in reality, did not concur on the *same* allegations interwoven into an over-broad article designed for just such a purpose.

F. The Article Fails to State an Impeachable Offense as a Matter of Law.

The Articles of Impeachment also fail because, as former D.C. Assistant Attorney General Jeffrey Scott Shapiro explains, "**The president didn't commit incitement or any other crime.**" As it relates to the allegation in the Article:

> In the District of Columbia, it's a crime to "intentionally or recklessly act in such a manner to cause another person to be in reasonable fear" and to "incite or provoke violence where there is a likelihood that such violence will ensue... The president didn't mention violence on Wednesday, much less provoke or incite it. He said, "I know that everyone here will soon be marching over to the Capitol building to peacefully and patriotically make your voices heard." District law defines a riot as "a public disturbance . . . which by tumultuous and violent conduct or the threat thereof creates grave danger of damage or injury to property or persons." When Mr. Trump spoke, there was no "public disturbance," only a rally. The "disturbance" came later at the Capitol by a small minority who entered the perimeter and broke the law. The president's critics want him charged for inflaming the emotions of angry Americans. That alone does not satisfy the elements of any criminal offense, and

> therefore his speech is protected by the Constitution that members of Congress are sworn to support and defend.[210]

It matters greatly that the President did not commit a crime, because the Constitutional requirement for action that is grounds for impeachment is a high crime or misdemeanor.

> By limiting impeachment to cases of "Treason, Bribery, or other high Crimes and Misdemeanors,"[211] the Framers restricted impeachment to specific offenses against "already known and established law."[212] That was a deliberate choice designed to constrain the impeachment power. In keeping with that restriction, every prior presidential impeachment in our history has been based on alleged violations of existing law—indeed, criminal law...[213] **The terminology of "high Crimes and Misdemeanors" makes clear that an impeachable offense must be a violation of established law.** The Impeachment Clause did not confer upon Congress a roving license to make up new standards of conduct for government officials and to permit removal from office merely on a conclusion that conduct was "bad" if there was not an existing law that it violated. [214]

House Democrats' theory on insurrection collapses at the threshold because it fails to describe any violation of law whatsoever. Aside from the decided lack of causation that the evidence *demonstrably* proves,[215] Mr. Trump's speech was well-within the long-understood protection of

---

210 Jeffrey Scott Shapiro, *No, Trump Isn't Guilty of Incitement*, Wall Street Journal (Jan. 10, 2021), https://www.wsj.com/articles/no-trump-isnt-guilty-of-incitement-11610303966

211 U.S. Const., art. II, § 4.

212 4 William Blackstone, *Commentaries on the Laws of England* *256.

213 *See Impeachment Inquiry into President Donald J. Trump: Constitutional Grounds for Presidential Impeachment Before the H.R. Comm. on the Judiciary*, 116th Cong. (2019) (written statement of Professor Jonathan Turley, Geo. Wash. Univ. Law Sch., at 15, https://perma.cc/QU4H-FZC4); H.R. Res. 611, 106th Cong. (1998); H.R. Comm. on the Judiciary, *Impeachment of William Jefferson Clinton, President of the United States*, H.R. Rep. No. 105-830, 105th Cong. 143 (1998) (additional views of Rep. Bill McCollum); H.R. Comm. on the Judiciary, *Impeachment of Richard M. Nixon, President of the United States*, H.R. Rep. No. 93-1305, 93d Cong. 1–3 (1974).

214 House Trial Memo 2020.

215 See timeline above and see FBI reports.

the First Amendment. A person does not lose his fundamental right to speak his mind just because he is the President.

IV. CONCLUSION

The Article of Impeachment presented by the House is unconstitutional for a variety of reasons, any of which alone would be grounds for immediate dismissal. Taken together, they demonstrate conclusively that indulging House Democrats hunger for this political theater is a danger to our Republic democracy and the rights that we hold dear. Reasons for dismissal include:

1. The Senate of the United States lacks jurisdiction over the 45th President because he holds no public office from which he can be removed, and the Constitution limits the authority of the Senate in cases of impeachment to removal from office as the prerequisite active remedy allowed the Senate under our Constitution.

2. The Senate of the United States lacks jurisdiction over the 45th President because he holds no public office from which he can be removed rendering the Article of Impeachment moot and a non-justiciable question.

3. Should the Senate act on the Article of Impeachment initiated in the House of Representatives, it will have passed a Bill of Attainder in violation of Article 1, Sec. 9. Cl. 3 of the United States Constitution.

4. The allegations in the Article of Impeachment are self-evidently wrong, as demonstrated by the evidence including the transcript of the President's actual speech, and the allegations fail to meet the constitutional standard for any crime, let alone an impeachable offense.

5. The House of Representatives deprived the 45th President of due process of law in rushing to issue the Article of Impeachment and by ignoring its own procedures and precedents going back to the mid-19th century. The lack of due process included, but was not limited to, its failure to conduct any meaningful committee review or other investigation, engage in any full and fair consideration of evidence in support of the Article, as well as the failure to conduct any full and fair discussion by allowing the 45th President's positions to be heard in the House Chamber. No exigent circumstances under the law were present excusing the House of Representatives' rush to judgment, as evidenced by the fact that they then held the Article for another 12 days.

6. The Article of Impeachment violates the 45th President's right to free speech and thought guaranteed under the First Amendment to the United States Constitution.

7. The Article is constitutionally flawed in that it charges multiple instances of allegedly impeachable conduct in a single article.

The Senate should dismiss these charges and acquit the President because this is clearly *not* what the Framers wanted or what the Constitution allows.

Respectfully submitted,

Bruce L. Castor, Jr.
David Schoen
Michael T. van der Veen
Counsel to the 45th President of the United States

February 8, 2021

This page intentionally left blank.

TABLE OF CONTENTS

TABLE OF CONTENTS

INTRODUCTION

President Trump's pre-trial brief confirms that he has no good defense of his incitement of an insurrection against the Nation he swore an oath to protect. Instead, he tries to shift the blame onto his supporters, and he invokes a set of flawed legal theories that would allow Presidents to incite violence and overturn the democratic process without fear of consequences. His brief—in which he refuses to accept responsibility for his actions—highlights the danger he continues to pose to the Nation he betrayed. To send a clear message to the Nation and to all future Presidents that efforts to undermine our democracy through violence will not be tolerated, the Senate should convict President Trump and disqualify him from ever holding office again.

President Trump's constitutional offense is a matter of public record that cannot be seriously disputed. After spending months propagating the lie that the 2020 election had been stolen from him, President Trump summoned his supporters to a rally in Washington on January 6. He seized on that date—when Congress and the Vice President were to hold a Joint Session to count the Electoral College votes—as his last chance to overturn the election and install himself in the White House for a second term against the will of the majority of Americans.

Against this backdrop, President Trump addressed a crowd that he knew was armed and primed for violence. He falsely raged to the crowd that the Joint Session was the culmination of a treasonous plot to destroy America. He exhorted his supporters to "fight like hell [or] you're not going to have a country anymore." And he urged the mob to march to the Capitol, telling them that "[y]ou'll never take back our country with weakness." He thus lit the match of insurrection and threw it into the powder keg he had spent months creating. President Trump now studiously

ignores all that preceded his speech and provided meaning and context to his statements, asking the Senate to do the same and focus only on a handful of his remarks in isolation.

There can be no doubt that President Trump is singularly responsible for inciting the violent insurrection that followed his speech. The mob he incited stormed the Capitol, bludgeoned the police with weapons, deployed chemical irritants, hunted Vice President Pence and Speaker Pelosi for their alleged "treason," and left threatening messages for Members of Congress—all the while proclaiming proudly that they were doing President Trump's bidding. By the end of the day, a police officer and four others were dead, dozens more were injured, and our Nation's Capitol was desecrated. As a direct result of President Trump's actions, the seat of our democracy has been transformed into a military camp. That is President Trump's legacy to the Nation.

Nor can there be any doubt that President Trump failed to act decisively to stop the violence as soon as it began. Instead, President Trump was "delighted" that the insurrection was delaying the counting of the Electoral College votes. In an astonishing act of further incitement and betrayal, President Trump denounced his own Vice President on Twitter *at the very time* the mob hunted him through the halls of the Capitol. When President Trump finally issued a statement after hours of delay, he blamed Congress for the attack on itself, and told the insurrectionists, "you're very special," and "we love you." Since then, he has described his conduct as "totally appropriate."

There can be no doubt that these facts amount to an impeachable offense. President Trump incited the insurrection while seeking to cheat in an election and remain in office for a second term against the will of America's voters. The Framers of our Constitution designed the impeachment power to protect against a President who would subvert our democracy to keep himself in power.

And the drafters of the Fourteenth Amendment further confirmed that an official who participates in an insurrection must be disqualified from future officeholding.[1] President Trump's conduct on January 6 was the paradigm of an impeachable offense.

Because President Trump's guilt is obvious, he seeks to evade responsibility for inciting the January 6 insurrection by arguing that the Senate lacks jurisdiction to convict officials after they leave office. This discredited argument has been rejected by scholars across the political spectrum, including many of the Nation's leading conservative constitutional lawyers, one of whom recently took to the pages of the Wall Street Journal to urge the Senate to accept jurisdiction over this trial. This argument has also been rejected by the very scholars on which President Trump principally relies, several of whom have taken *exactly the opposite position* as the position President Trump incorrectly ascribes to them in his trial memorandum. President Trump's jurisdictional argument is both wrong as a matter of constitutional law and dangerous as a matter of Senate practice. It would leave the Senate powerless to hold Presidents accountable for misconduct committed near the end of their terms. It would also create an obvious loophole in the Senate's disqualification power by allowing officials to resign immediately before their Senate trial. And it would encourage Presidents to commit abuses precisely when those abuses pose the greatest threat to our democracy—at election time. The Senate must reject this effort to eviscerate its impeachment power, just as it has rejected similar arguments in impeachments dating back more than 200 years.

President Trump's other defenses are equally weak. The First Amendment protects our democratic system—but it does not protect a President who incites his supporters to imperil that

[1] U.S. Const. amend. XIV, § 3.

system through violence. In the words of the Nation's leading First Amendment scholars, the argument that the First Amendment prevents the Senate from convicting the President is "legally frivolous."[2] Accepting President Trump's argument would mean that Congress could not impeach a President who burned an American flag on national television, or who spoke at a Ku Klux Klan rally in a white hood, or who wore a swastika while leading a march through a Jewish neighborhood—all of which is expression protected by the First Amendment but would obviously be grounds for impeachment. The First Amendment does not immunize President Trump from impeachment or limit the Senate's power to protect the Nation from an unfit leader. And even assuming the First Amendment applied, it would certainly not protect President Trump's speech on January 6, which incited lawless action.

President Trump's other purported defenses also fail. President Trump received all the process he was due. The House moved urgently to impeach him because he remained a danger after January 6. And President Trump's *trial* will occur in the Senate, which has provided for extensive pretrial briefing and an opportunity for him to present evidence before the Senate determines whether to convict. President Trump is also wrong to argue that he can only be impeached for a criminal violation. This argument has no support in history or precedent—and, once again, even the scholar on whom he relies has rejected it. Finally, President Trump's argument that the article of impeachment charges "multiple alleged wrongs" is simply false: the article charges a single course of impeachable conduct for inciting an insurrection.

* * *

---

[2] *Constitutional Law Scholars on President Trump's First Amendment Defense* at 1-2 (Feb. 5, 2021).

The question whether President Trump should be convicted and disqualified is not close. As the House Republican Conference Chair recognized, "There has never been a greater betrayal by a President of the United States of his office and his oath to the Constitution."[3] To deter future Presidents from attempting to subvert our Nation's elections, and to ensure that President Trump never again has an opportunity to endanger our democracy, the Senate should convict him and disqualify him from holding "any Office of honor, Trust or Profit under the United States."[4]

ARGUMENT

PRESIDENT TRUMP'S ATTEMPTED DEFENSES FAIL

Unable to defend his misconduct on January 6, President Trump devotes the majority of his brief to attempting to shift the blame to others, arguing that the Senate should not hold a trial at all, and trying to cloak his betrayal of the Nation in the First Amendment. All of his defenses fail.

A. President Trump Cannot Reasonably Deny Responsibility For Inciting The Insurrection

President Trump asserts that the insurrectionists stormed the Capitol "of their own accord and for their own reasons."[5] That argument defies belief. The factual record, as discussed in detail in our opening brief, demonstrates President Trump's singular responsibility for inciting the attack on the Capitol. That he does not like being held responsible by Congress does not allow him to rewrite history.

Before January 6, President Trump had tried and failed to overturn the election through every conceivable means at his disposal—flawed judicial challenges, threats against state officials,

---

[3] Liz Cheney, *I Will Vote To Impeach The President* (Jan. 12, 2021).
[4] U.S. Const., Art. I, § 3, cl. 7.
[5] Opp. at 9.

efforts to change state law, and even attempts to enlist his Attorney General to find proof of widespread fraud—all while he falsely insisted to his supporters that the election had been stolen from him.[6] After these methods failed, President Trump identified the Joint Session's electoral vote count as his final chance to retain his grip on the Presidency. He therefore planned a rally for the morning of January 6, just hours before Congress and the Vice President were to convene to affirm President Biden's election victory. He announced that he would personally appear at the rally, which he promoted constantly. The event "will be wild!"[7] he promised; a "historic day"[8] to "StopTheSteal!"[9]

By the morning of the rally, President Trump knew that many of his supporters, agitated by his barrage of lies about a stolen election, were prone to violence. An earlier pro-Trump rally in Washington, D.C. had ended in brawls, vandalism directed against churches, and numerous assaults on police officers.[10] One GOP election official even warned President Trump that his rhetoric

---

[6] William Cummings et al., *By the Numbers: President Donald Trump's Failed Efforts to Overturn the Election*, USA Today (Jan. 6, 2021); Michael Balsamo, *Disputing Trump, Barr Says No Widespread Election Fraud*, Associated Press (Dec. 1, 2020); Jesse Byrnes, *Barr Told Trump that Theories About Stolen Election Were "Bulls---": Report*, The Hill (Jan. 18, 2021); Amy Gardner & Paulina Firozi, *Here's the Full Transcript and Audio of the Call Between Trump and Raffensperger*, Wash. Post (Jan. 5, 2021); Maggie Haberman et al., *Trump Targets Michigan in His Ploy to Subvert the Election*, N.Y. Times (Nov. 19, 2020); Amy Gardner et al., *Trump Asks Pennsylvania House Speaker for Help Overturning Election Results, Personally Intervening in a Third State*, Wash. Post (Dec. 8, 2020); Ryan Randazzo et al., *Arizona Legislature 'Cannot and Will Not' Overturn Election, Republican House Speaker Says*, Arizona Republic (Dec. 4, 2020).

[7] Donald J. Trump (@realDonaldTrump), Twitter (Dec. 19, 2020, 1:42 AM).

[8] Donald J. Trump (@realDonaldTrump), Twitter (Jan. 3, 2021, 10:27 AM).

[9] Donald J. Trump (@realDonaldTrump), Twitter (Jan. 1, 2021, 2:53 PM).

[10] Peter Hermann & Keith Alexander, *Proud Boys Leader Barred From District By Judge Following His Arrest*, Wash. Post (Jan. 5, 2021); Jason Slotkin et al., *4 Stabbed, 33 Arrested After Trump Supporters, Counterprotesters Clash in D.C.*, NPR (Dec. 12, 2020); NBC Washington Staff, *4 Stabbed, 33 Arrested as Trump Supporters, Counterprotesters Clash in Downtown DC*, NBC Washington (Dec. 12, 2020).

would cause someone "to get killed."[11] When he stood at the podium before thousands of his supporters, President Trump knew that they were armed and that they were angry.

President Trump then whipped his followers into a frenzy. He launched into an impassioned attack on a "stolen election"[12]—falsely telling the crowd that Congress's actions at the Joint Session would be the culmination of a vast conspiracy to destroy the country. And President Trump made clear what he wanted them to do: go to the Capitol and "fight like hell." He told the crowd to march to the Capitol, even falsely pledging to join them on the march. He told them that "if you don't fight like hell you're not going to have a country anymore."[13] He added: "you'll never take back our country with weakness."[14]

President Trump cannot credibly claim that he is not responsible for what followed. As Leader McConnell accurately put it, "[t]he mob was fed lies" and "provoked by the president."[15] The insurrectionists themselves made clear that they understood that they were following President Trump's commands—they proudly said so in videos taken as they ransacked the Capitol, in statements to reporters after the riot, and in court when attempting to explain their heinous actions.[16] The many American flags wielded by attackers demonstrated that they believed they were performing a patriotic act in the service of their President. The rioters attacked the Capitol because

---

11 Stephen Fowler, *'Someone's Going To Get Killed': Ga. Official Blasts GOP Silence On Election Threats*, NPR (Dec. 1, 2020).

12 Donald J. Trump (@realDonaldTrump), Twitter (Nov. 8, 2020, 9:17 AM).

13 *Watch LIVE: Save America March at The Ellipse featuring President @realDonaldTrump*, RSBN TV (Jan. 6, 2021); *Donald Trump Speech "Save America" Rally Transcript January 6*, Rev (Jan. 6, 2021).

14 *Id.*

15 Mike DeBonis & Paul Kane, *Uncertainty Reigns in Senate as Schumer Pushes Fast Agenda and McConnell Calls Out Trump*, Wash. Post (Jan. 19, 2021).

16 Zoe Tillman, *Trump Supporters' Own Explanations For Assaulting The Capitol Are Undercutting His Impeachment Defense*, BuzzFeed News (Feb. 2, 2021); House Trial Mem. at 27-28.

President Trump plied them with false assertions that Congress and the Vice President were in the process of stealing their democracy.

President Trump argues that he "did not direct anyone to commit lawless actions,"[17] but as the crowd well knew, he had been urging Vice President Pence to do just that: by unilaterally and unconstitutionally overturning the election results at the Joint Session. President Trump's unsuccessful attempt to pressure Vice President Pence into acting unlawfully surely inspired the mob to believe that it needed to attack the Capitol—and to hunt down the Vice President himself when he refused.

If, as President Trump suggests, the mob "completely misunderstood him,"[18] and if he disapproved of the violence perpetrated by those who purported to act in his name, he could have acted swiftly to set them straight. But he refused. Instead, he was "delighted" by the riot at the Capitol because he believed it increased his chances of overturning the election. He even tweeted an attack on his own Vice President while the riot was underway.[19] Only after receiving public and private entreaties did he issue a pair of lukewarm tweets asking his supporters to "[s]tay peaceful" even as they committed horrific violence.[20] Finally, *three hours* after the siege began, he released a scripted video telling insurrectionists "We love you, you're very special. … I know how you feel."[21] Even then, he insisted that the election was "stolen from us"[22]—the same lie that had incited his

[17] Opp. at 11.
[18] Opp. at 11.
[19] Donald J. Trump (@realDonaldTrump), Twitter (Jan. 6, 2021, 2:24 PM).
[20] Donald J. Trump (@realDonaldTrump), Twitter (Jan. 6, 2021, 2:38 PM).
[21] Donald J. Trump (@realDonaldTrump), Twitter (Jan. 6, 2021, 4:17 PM); *President Trump Video Statement on Capitol Protestors*, C-SPAN (Jan. 6, 2021).
[22] *Id.*

supporters to commit violence in the first place. And in the evening, after the insurrection was finally put down, he blamed it on Congress: "These are the things and events that happen when a sacred landslide election victory is so unceremoniously & viciously stripped away from great patriots who have been badly & unfairly treated for so long."[23] President Trump barely attempts to justify his abject failure to stop the riot after it began, and confines his entire discussion of the point to a convoluted footnote that hardly offers any response or explanation at all.[24]

President Trump only *increases* his own responsibility by pointing to indications that some of the attackers planned the insurrection "*several days* in advance of the rally."[25] That fact underscores that President Trump knew exactly what he was doing in his campaign to overturn the election. Any plans hatched in advance were intended to support President Trump, who had inflamed his followers and invited them to converge in Washington, D.C., on January 6 to "StoptheSteal." His continued insistence that he was the rightful winner of the election was the oxygen that enabled their plans to flourish. And his incendiary remarks at the rally itself, delivered despite warnings that the crowd was poised and prepared for violence at his instigation, were the match that detonated everything. Had he accepted the verdict of the Electoral College—like *every* presidential candidate before him—there would have been no plans, no rally, no calls to "fight," and no insurrection.

Finally, President Trump does not help his case by arguing that his January 6 speech was intended to encourage his supporters to press for "election security generally."[26] To call this argument implausible would be an act of charity. The rally, set for the day when Congress was to

---

[23] Donald J. Trump (@realDonaldTrump), Twitter (Jan. 6, 2021, 6:01 PM).
[24] Opp. at 3 n.8.
[25] Opp. at 8.
[26] Opp. at 52.

count the electoral votes, was the culmination of President Trump's months-long campaign to overturn the results of a *specific* election he lost. In his speech, President Trump did not direct his supporters to go home and lobby their state legislatures, but instead directed them to march to the Capitol and fight. President Trump's speech did not promote election security—it exhorted a mob to attack Congress in order to overturn a free and fair election.

B. The Senate Has Jurisdiction To Try This Impeachment

President Trump is wrong to cast doubt on the Senate's jurisdiction over this trial. Scholars from across the political spectrum, including renowned conservative constitutional scholars, have recognized that the Constitution empowers the Senate to convict and disqualify officials who commit misconduct late in their terms and therefore can realistically only be tried after leaving office. We thus explained in our opening brief that there is no "January Exception."

As the former Reagan Administration official Chuck Cooper recently wrote in the Wall Street Journal, scholarship regarding the Senate's jurisdiction "has matured substantially" since this body voted on that question.[27] This scholarship "has exposed the serious weakness" in President Trump's claim that the Senate lacks jurisdiction.[28] For the reasons given by Cooper and others, Senators who previously voted to reject jurisdiction over this trial might wish to "reconsider their view and judge the former president's misconduct on the merits."[29]

<u>*Constitutional Text:*</u> President Trump's brief glaringly fails to address the constitutional text that establishes the Senate's jurisdiction over this trial. The language of the Constitution gives the

---

[27] Chuck Cooper, *The Constitution Doesn't Bar Trump's Impeachment Trial*, Wall Street Journal (Feb. 7, 2021).
[28] *Id.*
[29] *Id.*

Senate "the sole Power to try all Impeachments"[30]—not just impeachments involving sitting officials. As noted by Michael McConnell, a prominent scholar and former court of appeals judge appointed by President George W. Bush, the key word in the Constitutional text is "all."[31] "This clause contains no reservation or limitation" and it does not "say the Senate has power to try impeachments against sitting officers."[32] The constitutional text thus "makes clear that the Senate has power to try th[is] impeachment."[33]

The Senate's jurisdiction in this case is especially clear given that the House undisputedly had jurisdiction to impeach President Trump while he was still President. Regardless of whether the *House* would have the authority to commence an impeachment proceeding against an official after he left office, the *Senate* plainly has authority to try the impeachment of an official like President Trump who was still in office when he was impeached. Indeed, President Trump's attorneys attempt to support their jurisdictional argument by citing scholars who have said exactly the opposite of what President Trump ascribes to them; they have confirmed that the Senate possesses jurisdiction in these circumstances. For example, one article that President Trump relies on[34] concludes: "as long as an officer served in office at the time formal impeachment proceedings started, then the House and Senate retain jurisdiction to continue the process because the officer was 'in office' at the

---

[30] U.S. Const., Art. I, § 3, cl. 6.

[31] Eugene Volokh, *Impeaching Officials While They're in Office, but Trying Them After They Leave*, The Volokh Conspiracy (Jan. 28, 2021) (quoting Prof. Michael McConnell).

[32] *Id.*

[33] *Id.*

[34] Opp. at 19, 31, 36.

commencement of the proceedings."[35] Another scholar that President Trump repeatedly cites[36] recently opined: "Trump's defenders will surely contend that a president cannot be tried by the Senate after he has left office. They are wrong."[37] President Trump's brief's serious distortion of these scholars' views is deeply troubling.

Rather than tackle the Senate's unqualified power to try *all* impeachments or accurately represent the scholarship on this question, President Trump instead mistakenly invokes other constitutional provisions that he claims limit the Senate's power by implication. He cites the provision of Article I stating that "Judgment in Cases of Impeachment shall not extend further than to removal from Office, and disqualification to hold and enjoy any Office of honor, Trust or Profit under the United States."[38] This provision means that the Senate may not impose judgments that "extend further" than (1) removal of the accused if he remains in office, and (2) disqualification of the accused regardless of whether he remains in office. But nothing in this provision confines the Senate's disqualification power to cases involving sitting officials.

President Trump argues that because only sitting officials are subject to the removal remedy, then *only* sitting officials should be subject to the separate disqualification remedy.[39] But this argument attempts to add a word to the Constitutional text—"only"—that the Framers omitted. It also defies logic. If a law sets out two possible penalties and one of them becomes unavailable, that

---

[35] Harold J. Krent, *Can President Trump Be Impeached As Mr. Trump? Exploring the Temporal Dimension of Impeachments*, 95 Chi.-Kent L. Rev. 537, 548 (2021) (emphasis added).

[36] Opp. at 17, 20-21.

[37] Brian C. Kalt & Frank Bowman, *Congress Can Impeach Trump Now and Convict Him When He's Gone*, Wash. Post (Jan. 11, 2021). Professor Kalt has noted that, in several places, President Trump's brief contains "multiple . . . flat-out misrepresentations" of his scholarship. Brian Kalt (@ProfBrianKalt), Twitter (Feb. 8, 2021, 11:57 AM).

[38] U.S. Const., Art. I, § 3, cl. 7.

[39] Opp. at 30.

does not mean that the offender is exempt from the penalty that remains. Consider the example of a "con man" convicted under a statute that provides for both mandatory refund of the proceeds of his crime as well as a prison term. Even if the "con man" spends all the proceeds of his crime before his trial, thus making the refund penalty unavailable, he is obviously still subject to the penalty of imprisonment.[40]

President Trump also cites the provision of Article II stating that "The President, Vice President and all civil Officers of the United States, shall be removed from Office" upon impeachment and conviction.[41] This provision means that sitting officials who are impeached and convicted must be removed from office. But, as Cooper explains, this provision "cuts *against*" the theory that the Senate lacks jurisdiction over former officials.[42] Instead, this provision "simply establishes what is known in criminal law as a 'mandatory minimum' punishment: If an incumbent officeholder is convicted by a two-thirds vote of the Senate, he is removed from office as a matter of law."[43] It does not exempt former officials, and it certainly does not support the illogical leap that former officials are altogether immune from the Senate's power to try all impeachments.

The Constitution itself makes clear that the category of officials who can be tried in the Senate is broader than the category of "civil officers" who must be removed from office upon conviction. When the Constitution refers to the full category of individuals who can be tried by the Senate, it refers to "persons" and "parties"[44]—a broader category than the sitting "civil officers"

---

[40] *See* Frank O. Bowman, III, *The Constitutionality of Trying a Former President Impeached While in Office*, Lawfare (Feb. 3, 2021).

[41] Opp. at 18; U.S. Const., Art. II, § 4.

[42] Chuck Cooper, *The Constitution Doesn't Bar Trump's Impeachment Trial*, Wall Street Journal (Feb. 7, 2021).

[43] *Id.*

[44] U.S. Const., Art. I, § 3, cl. 6, 7.

subject to mandatory removal. President Trump does not even attempt to answer this point. Notably, President Trump filed a lengthy brief, but failed to engage with key jurisdictional arguments grounded in the Constitution's actual text.

President Trump next cites the provision stating that "When the President of the United States is tried, the Chief Justice shall preside."[45] This provision requires the Chief Justice to preside over the impeachment trial of a sitting President. But Donald Trump is not a sitting President, which means that the Chief Justice need not preside at his trial—just as the Chief Justice does not preside over impeachment trials of other officials. The Framers required the Chief Justice to preside over the trial of a sitting President to ensure that the Vice President, as President of the Senate, does not oversee a trial where conviction would result in her ascending to the presidency. That concern is not implicated in a trial of a former President.

Finally, President Trump wrongly suggests that, because he is now a private citizen, convicting and disqualifying him would raise concerns under the Bill of Attainder Clause, which prohibits Congress from following the old English practice of passing laws that single out a specific individual for punishment.[46] But unlike in the Supreme Court cases cited by President Trump,[47] which involved legislative attempts to punish individuals for their private conduct, President Trump was impeached by the House while he was in office for abuses he committed as a sitting President. He does not even try to claim that the House lacked authority to impeach him for those abuses.

---

[45] Opp. at 23; U.S. Const., Art. I, § 3, cl. 6.
[46] *See* Opp. at 15-17; *see also* U.S. Const., Art. I, § 9, cl. 3.
[47] Opp. at 16-17.

Trying, convicting, and disqualifying him in the Senate based on those same abuses poses no risk of subjecting a private party to punitive legislative action targeting his private conduct.

__History__: The "originalist" case for the Senate's jurisdiction here could hardly be stronger. President Trump does not dispute that the Framers looked to English practice as a model for the federal impeachment power. And President Trump concedes that, in the English system, officials could be impeached and disqualified after leaving office.[48] In fact, as we described in our opening brief (at 51), Warren Hastings, a former official, faced impeachment charges in England even as the Framers gathered in Philadelphia to draft our Constitution—and the Framers cited his case as one in which impeachment was appropriate. President Trump is therefore left to make the implausible argument that the Framers intended to depart from this settled English practice without saying so.

President Trump similarly concedes that numerous state constitutions during the founding era provided for the impeachment of former officials.[49] None prohibited such impeachments. Indeed, in some states, *only* former officials could be impeached, which confirms that the Framers surely understood that the impeachment power could also encompass former officials. Had they intended to depart from that understanding, they would have said so.

Precedent dating back more than 200 years makes the Senate's jurisdiction here even clearer—as noted by, among many others, Professor Steven Calabresi, Co-Chairman of the Federalist Society's Board of Directors.[50] After leaving office, President John Quincy Adams recognized that he was "amenable to impeachment by [the] House for everything I did during the

[48] Opp. at 20.
[49] Opp. at 21.
[50] Steven G. Calabresi and Norman Eisen, *We Disagree on a Lot. But We Both Think Trump Should Be Convicted*, N.Y. Times (Jan. 13, 2021).

time I held any public office."[51] And the Senate has several times affirmed that it has the power to try, convict, and disqualify officials after they leave office. When Senator Blount was expelled from the Senate after being impeached in 1798, he expressly disavowed at his Senate trial the radical claim (made here by President Trump) that former officials were categorically exempt from trial.[52]

When Secretary of War Belknap was impeached in 1876 shortly after resigning, the Senate squarely rejected his argument that there was no jurisdiction to try him as a former official.[53] President Trump asserts that the Senate's exercise of jurisdiction in the Belknap trial should not be treated as precedent because Belknap was ultimately acquitted. But before Belknap was acquitted, the Senate rejected the exact same jurisdictional claim that President Trump presses here.[54] President Trump relies at length on Joseph Story to support that now-rejected claim.[55] But Story's conclusions were equivocal—indeed, he recognized that impeachment of former officers could still serve a purpose because "a judgment of disqualification might still be pronounced."[56]

If there were any doubt on the question, when the House impeached Judge Archbald in 1912, based in part on his conduct in a prior judgeship, "a majority of the [S]enators voting saw no

---

[51] Cong. Globe, 29th Cong., 1st Sess. 641 (1846).

[52] Eleanore Bushnell, *Crimes, Follies, and Misfortunes: The Federal Impeachment Trials*, at 30 (1992).

[53] Brian C. Kalt, *The Constitutional Case for the Impeachability of Former Federal Officials: An Analysis of the Law, History, and Practice of Late Impeachment*, 6 Tex. Rev. L. & Pol. 13, 96 (2001).

[54] Opp. at 25-26. President Trump also points to opinions by Nebraska and Florida courts regarding their states' impeachment power. *See* Opp. at 28-30. But the Nebraska case involved an officer who had left office before the impeachment investigation even began, and the court found under state law that while a former officer could not be impeached and tried, a former officer could be tried if he had been in office at the time of his impeachment. *See State v. Hill*, 55 N.W. 794, 795, 798 (Neb. 1893); *see also* Opp. 34 n.86. In any event, the opinions of *state* courts interpreting *state* law in cases decided a century or two after the federal Constitution was drafted are not persuasive evidence of the scope of the federal impeachment power.

[55] Opp. at 31-32.

[56] Joseph Story, *Commentaries on the Constitution of the United States* § 801 (R. Rotunda & J. Nowak eds., 1987); *see also* Brian C. Kalt, *The Constitutional Case for the Impeachability of Former Federal Officials: An Analysis of the Law, History, and Practice of Late Impeachment*, 6 Tex. Rev. L. & Pol. 13, 123 (2001).

problem" with impeaching him for misconduct in his former office.[57] In more than 200 years, the Senate has *never* accepted the self-defeating argument that it lacks the power to try the impeachment of a former official. The Senate should not do so for the first time now.

Purpose of Impeachment: Once again failing to engage with the Constitution's plain text, President Trump argues that "[t]he purpose of impeachment is to remove someone from office."[58] But removal is not the only purpose of impeachment. In crafting the impeachment power, the Framers included two separate remedies—removal from office *as well as* disqualification from future officeholding. Distinct from the removal power, the disqualification power was intended to ensure that officials who abused their power were never again permitted to attain office from which they could threaten the American people. This animating purpose of disqualification—to protect the Nation from the return of a dangerous official—applies just as forcefully when the official has left office by the time the Senate tries his impeachment. President Trump does not even attempt to explain why the Framers would have provided that a *sitting* President found to have endangered the Nation should be disqualified from returning to office, but a *former* President found to have done the exact same thing should be free to return.

Nor can President Trump defend the perverse consequences that would result from his theory. The Framers feared more than anything a President who spared "no efforts or means whatever to get himself re-elected."[59] Thus, they understood that the paradigm case for impeachment would arise from a President's efforts to overturn an election. But elections, by

---

[57] *Id.* at 104.
[58] Opp. at 18.
[59] 2 The Records of the Federal Convention of 1787, at 64 (Max Farrand, ed., 1911).

definition, occur at the end of a President's term. It is inconceivable that the Framers designed impeachment to be virtually useless in a President's final weeks or days, when opportunities to interfere with the peaceful transfer of power are most present. And it is equally inconceivable that the Framers intended to create a remedy that would make no sense: disqualify a President from future office if he tried and succeeded to overturn an election, thus remaining in office, but not if—like President Trump—he tried and failed.

The consequences of President Trump's jurisdictional argument get more dangerous still. President Trump does not dispute that, if his theory were correct, the Senate would be powerless to address abuse by officials that comes to light only after they leave office. Nor does President Trump dispute that, under his theory, a President "who betrayed the public trust and was impeached could avoid accountability simply by resigning one minute before the Senate's final conviction vote."[60] The President could thus evade the Senate's disqualification power by resigning, then could later return to office, where he would be free to betray the public trust all over again. This loophole would "practically annihilate the power of impeachment in all cases of guilt clearly provable."[61]

President Trump points out that Congress in the past has declined to impeach, convict, and disqualify officials after they leave office. President Trump asks why, for example, the House did not impeach President Nixon after he resigned.[62] The answer is that impeachment, conviction, and disqualification were unnecessary where President Nixon resigned in disgrace, acknowledged wrongdoing, and was already barred from running again for President by the Twenty-Second

---

[60] *Constitutional Law Scholars on Impeaching Former Officers* at 2 (Jan. 21, 2021).
[61] 4 Cong. Rec. at 79 (1876) (Opinion of Senator Thurman).
[62] Opp. at 27.

Amendment.[63] By contrast, President Trump has described his conduct as "totally appropriate,"[64] refused to accept responsibility for his abuses, and is eligible to seek the Presidency—and assault the democratic process—yet again.

That Congress has previously found it unnecessary to disqualify former officials despite its clear power to do so demonstrates that Congress does not take this step lightly. It also demonstrates that there is no merit to President Trump's spurious claim that disqualifying him here would open the floodgates and allow Congress to use impeachments to pursue old grudges or settle old scores—particularly given that President Trump was still in office when he was impeached.[65] And, above all else, it highlights the unprecedented danger created by President Trump's effort to cling to power by inciting an attack on Congress. The Senate must reject President Trump's invitation to eviscerate one of the Senate's most important tools for protecting the Nation against officials who attempt to subvert our democracy.

C. The First Amendment Provides No Defense to Conviction and Disqualification

President Trump's reliance on the First Amendment is an insult to the values that the First Amendment enshrines. In the words of nearly 150 First Amendment lawyers and constitutional scholars, President Trump's First Amendment defense is "legally frivolous."[66]

---

[63] *See* President Nixon's Resignation Speech, August 8, 1974; *see also* U.S. Const. amend. XXII ("No person shall be elected to the office of the President more than twice . . .").

[64] Kevin Liptak & Betsy Klein, *Defiant Trump Denounces Violence but Takes No Responsibility for Inciting Deadly Riot,* CNN (Jan. 12, 2021).

[65] Opp. at 35.

[66] *Constitutional Law Scholars on President Trump's First Amendment Defense* at 1-2 (Feb. 5, 2021); *see also* Nicholas Fandos et al., *144 Constitutional Lawyers Call Trump's First Amendment Defense 'Legally Frivolous,'* N.Y. Times (Feb. 5, 2021).

President Trump argues that he is "protected by the First Amendment" "[l]ike all Americans."[67] He is wrong from the beginning: the President is not "[l]ike all Americans." The First Amendment has no application in an impeachment proceeding, which does not seek to punish unlawful speech, but instead to protect the Nation from a President who violated his oath of office and abused the public trust.

Under President Trump's view of the First Amendment, even a sitting President who strenuously urged States to secede from the Union and rebel against the federal government would be immune from impeachment. Likewise, a President could declare his loyalty to a foreign power or publicly renounce his oath "to preserve, protect, and defend the Constitution"—all without fear of impeachment.[68] The First Amendment provides no such immunity for a President who has committed "high Crimes and Misdemeanors."

In fact, the Senate has confirmed that the First Amendment does not limit its power to convict in an impeachment proceeding. In 1804, the Senate convicted Judge John Pickering in part for inflammatory and politically charged statements he made from the bench.[69] No precedent supports President Trump's contrary view. He cites the impeachment of President Johnson in 1868, contending that the Senate there established that a President cannot be convicted and disqualified

---

[67] Answer at 4-5, 10; Opp. at 37-66.

[68] *See Constitutional Law Scholars on President Trump's First Amendment Defense* at 1; *see also* Peter D. Keisler & Richard D. Bernstein, *Freedom of Speech Doesn't Mean What Trump's Lawyers Want It to Mean*, The Atlantic (Feb. 2021) (arguing that President Trump's First Amendment argument is wrong and could produce the absurd result that a President could not be impeached if he or she "burned an American flag on national television to demonstrate contempt for the country he or she had been chosen to lead" or "wore a swastika while leading a Nazi march through a Jewish neighborhood").

[69] Keith E. Whittington, *Is There a Free Speech Defense to an Impeachment?*, Lawfare (Jan. 19, 2021).

based on his speech.[70] But the Senate set no such precedent in President Johnson's impeachment. As President Trump notes, one of the articles of impeachment charged President Johnson with insulting and denouncing Congress by "mak[ing] and declar[ing] … certain intemperate, inflammatory, and scandalous harangues … [which] are peculiarly indecent and unbecoming in the Chief Magistrate of the United States."[71] While some Senators expressed concern that President Johnson's remarks were constitutionally protected,[72] others disagreed. Senator Jacob Howard, for example, stated that "[n]o question of the 'freedom of speech' arises here."[73] Ultimately the Senate never voted on the article and thus made no judgment about the relevance of the First Amendment. In any event, there is no comparison between President Johnson's "intemperate" broadsides and President Trump's incitement of an insurrection.

Indeed, even if—contrary to precedent and scholarship—the First Amendment were understood to restrict Congress's power over impeachments, it still would not protect President Trump's calls to violence.[74] In *Brandenburg v. Ohio*, the Supreme Court explained that, while the First Amendment prohibits states from punishing "mere advocacy," it does *not* preclude punishment for speech that is "is directed to inciting or producing imminent lawless action and is likely to incite or produce such action."[75] President Trump's speech falls squarely within this exception for incitement. His statements on January 6, particularly in the context of his prior remarks, were

---

[70] Opp. at 65-66.

[71] *The Impeachment of Andrew Johnson (1868) President of the United States*, U.S. Senate, www.senate.gov/artandhistory/history/common/briefing/Impeachment_Johnson.htm#7.

[72] 3 Trial of Andrew Johnson 206 (1868) (speech of Sen. Joseph Fowler).

[73] *Id.* at 49 (speech of Sen. Jacob Howard).

[74] *Brandenburg v. Ohio*, 395 U.S. 444, 449 (1969).

[75] *Id.* at 447.

"directed to" and "likely to incite or produce" imminent unlawful action.[76] President Trump incited a crowd to go to the Capitol and fight, immediately before they stormed the Capitol.

These statements would not be protected whether they were made by an elected official, a civil servant, or a private citizen—contrary to President Trump's lengthy argument that those distinctions should matter.[77] President Trump is not helped by his reliance on a case concerning punishment for statements made by an elected official "as a private citizen" that "did not present a danger to the administration of justice."[78] Nor does the Supreme Court's recognition that an elected legislator could not be excluded from state office for "criticizing public policy" advance President Trump's claim, where the Court distinguished that situation from one in which "a legislator swears to an oath pro forma while … manifesting his … indifference to the oath."[79] President Trump's speech was not a criticism of public policy—rather, it was a repudiation of his oath of office as he incited a violent insurrection and then manifested callous indifference to its deadly consequences.

President Trump attempts to equate his January 6 speech to statements by other politicians, arguing that convicting him will chill political speech.[80] But context matters under the First Amendment. While other political figures have used heated rhetoric, none of the speeches that President Trump cites bears any resemblance to President Trump's anti-democratic effort to prolong his presidency by exhorting a mob to attack the Congress. President Trump spoke to

---

[76] *Constitutional Law Scholars on President Trump's First Amendment Defense* at 2-3 (concluding that President Trump's "words and conduct were not protected" under the First Amendment because they were "in the words of the *Brandenburg* case, 'directed to inciting or producing imminent lawless action and … likely to … produce such action'").

[77] Opp. at 41-46 (citing *Wood v. Georgia*, 370 U.S. 375 (1962), and *Bond v. Floyd*, 385 U.S. 116 (1966)).

[78] *See Wood*, 370 U.S. at 382, 393, 395.

[79] *Bond*, 385 U.S. at 132, 136.

[80] Opp. at 63-64.

supporters who were angry, prepared for violence, and intent on disrupting Congress's counting of the electoral votes. Knowing all that, he launched into an inflammatory speech that was bound to result in the violence that followed. And, of great significance, as his supporters overtook the Capitol, instead of acting to stop them, he watched delightedly on television, continued to disparage his Vice President, and lobbied Senators to overturn the election. That conduct is impeachable.

D. President Trump Has Received From Congress All The Process He Was Due

President Trump's claim that the House denied him due process by moving too quickly to impeach him has no grounding in law or fact. It also misunderstands the constitutional process for impeachments: his impeachment *trial* occurs in the Senate, not in the House.

The Constitution vests the House with the "sole Power of Impeachment"[81] and the power to "determine the Rules of its Proceedings."[82] Here, the House had to move quickly to address President Trump's dangerous misconduct, to discourage him from engaging in further abuse during the last days of his term, and to send an immediate signal that such an attack on our core democratic institutions will not be tolerated. And it was appropriate for the House to impeach without a lengthy investigation because the most relevant evidence against him is a matter of undisputed public record—the underlying events played out on live television and social media and were witnessed firsthand by Members of Congress.

President Trump ignores reality in arguing that there was no exigency that justified the House's urgent impeachment of him.[83] His actions after January 6 established that he posed a

---

[81] U.S. Const., Art. I, § 2, cl. 5.
[82] U.S. Const., Art. I, § 5, cl. 2.
[83] Opp. at 68-71.

continuing, immediate threat to our democracy. When the House impeached him one week after the insurrection, it was rightly concerned that "a President capable of fomenting a violent insurrection in the Capitol is capable of greater dangers still."[84] Importantly, President Trump had failed to show any remorse for the violence and instead continued to fan the flames.[85]

In light of this ongoing threat, five days after the assault on the Capitol, an article of impeachment was introduced in the House and referred to the House Committee on the Judiciary. During a hearing the following day, the Chairman of the Judiciary Committee submitted a 50-page report documenting the Committee's findings supporting impeachment, relying heavily on recorded speeches and actions.[86] One day later—on January 13, 2021—the House voted to impeach President Trump with bipartisan support on charges that he incited an insurrection. The article of impeachment was adopted with the support of 232 House Members, including every Democrat and ten Republicans.[87] This House impeachment provided President Trump with all the process he was due.

President Trump now argues that the House did not need to act expeditiously because his term ended without "apocalyptic predictions … coming to pass."[88] That ignores the fact that the impeachment itself limited the danger posed by President Trump. The House sent a clear message

---

[84] *House Judiciary Committee Majority Staff Report: Materials in Support of H. Res. 24, Impeaching Donald John Trump, President of the United States, for High Crimes and Misdemeanors*, at 3, 117th Cong (Jan. 12, 2021).

[85] *See id.* at 40-43.

[86] *House Judiciary Committee Majority Staff Report: Materials in Support of H. Res. 24, Impeaching Donald John Trump, President of the United States, for High Crimes and Misdemeanors*, 117th Cong (Jan. 12, 2021).

[87] Clerk of the U.S. House of Representatives, Roll Call 17, H. Res. 24 (Jan. 13, 2021).

[88] Opp. at 69.

that the President's conduct would not be tolerated, and President Trump was undoubtedly chastened in the final days of his term, knowing that he would face a Senate impeachment trial.

For these reasons, there was no procedural flaw in the House's impeachment of President Trump. But even if there were, that would be irrelevant to the Senate's separate exercise of its "sole Power *to try* all Impeachments."[89] Any defect in the House's impeachment proceedings—which are not an impeachment trial—could be cured when the evidence is presented to the Senate at trial.

President Trump incorrectly suggests that the Senate is like an appellate court, reviewing the decision of a lower court.[90] But that is not how the Framers structured the impeachment power: the House has the sole power to impeach, and the Senate has the sole power to try the impeachment and convict. It is the constitutional duty of *the Senate* to consider the evidence and decide for itself whether President Trump is guilty of inciting an insurrection. And President Trump has been provided with every opportunity to defend himself in his Senate trial, including additional time to prepare, extensive pretrial briefing,[91] and the opportunity to testify, which he declined.[92]

President Trump mistakenly points to the timing of the Senate impeachment trial to insist that there was no exigency in the House's impeachment. But the timing of the Senate trial was negotiated by leaders from both parties. Indeed, "Senate Republicans had requested *more time* to

---

[89] U.S. Const., Art. I, § 3, cl. 6 (emphasis added).
[90] Opp. at 70.
[91] S. Res. 16, 117th Cong. (2021).
[92] *See* Ltr. from Representative Raskin to President Trump (Feb. 4, 2021) (inviting President Trump to provide testimony); Ltr. from Bruce Castor to Representative Raskin (Feb. 4, 2021) (declining invitation).

allow Trump's lawyers to prepare."[93] The Senate then passed a resolution providing that the trial would begin on February 9, 2021.[94]

Finally, the allegation that Senator Leahy will be biased in presiding over the impeachment trial is both offensive and mistaken.[95] As Senator Leahy has explained: "I consider holding the office of the president pro tempore and the responsibilities that come with it to be one of the highest honors and most serious responsibilities of my career. When I preside over the impeachment trial of former President Donald Trump, I will not waver from my constitutional and sworn obligations to administer the trial with fairness, in accordance with the Constitution and the laws."[96]

E. The Senate Is Not Limited To The Standards Of Criminal Law

President Trump mistakenly contends that conviction by the Senate is only permitted where the House charges a violation of criminal law.[97] Under President Trump's view of the Senate's power to try impeachments, even if every Senator found that all of the allegations in the article were true, the Senate could not convict because the article does not specifically "describe any violation of law."[98] As Chuck Cooper recently put it, the argument that the alleged conduct does not rise to the level of an impeachable offense is "a hard argument to make with a straight face."[99] And as Steven

---

[93] Dartunorro Clark, *House Managers Deliver Impeachment Article Against Trump, Kicking Off Trial Preparations*, NBC News (Jan. 25, 2021) (emphasis added); Mike DeBonis, *Senate Ends Standoff, Agrees to Start Trump's Impeachment Trial Feb. 9*, Wash. Post (Jan. 22, 2021).

[94] S. Res. 16, 117th Cong. (2021).

[95] *See* Opp. at 70.

[96] Senator Patrick Leahy, Comment on Presiding Over the Impeachment Trial of President Donald Trump (Jan. 25, 2021).

[97] Opp. at 26, 72-74.

[98] Opp. at 73.

[99] Chuck Cooper, *The Constitution Doesn't Bar Trump's Impeachment Trial*, Wall Street Journal (Feb. 7, 2021).

Calabresi explained, "Whether or not Trump's words were a violation of the criminal law, they fall squarely within the Framers' definition of 'a High Crime and Misdemeanor.'"[100] Although President Trump's conduct may separately violate the criminal code, impeachment is not limited to criminal offenses, nor is it governed by the standards of proof that may apply in a criminal trial.[101] Indeed, even the legal scholar on whom President Trump relies has previously acknowledged that impeachment has never been understood to require criminal conduct.[102] The House therefore was not required to charge—and the Senate need not find—that President Trump committed any criminal offense.

Impeachment was conceived in the English Parliament as a method to control the King's ministers. It was not limited to accusations of criminal wrongdoing, but instead included broader, non-criminal offenses including abuse of power, corruption, and neglect of duty.[103] The Framers were aware of this history and understood that impeachment and conviction must reach a broad array of conduct beyond criminal misconduct, including abuse of power, betrayal of the Nation, and

---

[100] Steve Calabresi, *Trump Should Be Convicted By The Senate*, Daily Caller (Jan. 28, 2021).

[101] *See* H. Rep. No. 116-346 at 56-62.

[102] *See* Jonathan Turley, Written Statement, *The Impeachment Inquiry into President Donald J. Trump: The "Constitutional Basis" for Presidential Impeachment*, at 10-11 (Dec. 4, 2019) (acknowledging that, since the Founding, it has been understood that impeachable acts need not constitute criminal offenses); *see also Constitutional Law Scholars on President Trump's First Amendment Defense* at 1 (Feb. 5, 2021) (explaining that "Congress's power to impeach is not limited to *unlawful* acts" and that "violations of an officer's oath of office can constitute impeachable 'high Crimes or misdemeanors' under the Constitution even if no law has been violated"); Alan Dershowitz, *The Case Against Impeaching Trump*, at 26-27 (2018) (conceding that, if it were true that impeachment were warranted only for criminal law violations, it would lead to the absurd results that the President could not be impeached even if he allowed an enemy power to invade and conquer American territory). President Trump also mistakenly cites Professor Paul Campos, apparently to support his argument about what conduct is impeachable. Opp. at 66 n.195. But Professor Campos's article addressed a different subject—the standard for removing a sitting President under the Twenty-Fifth Amendment—and, in any event, he has since confirmed that it does not stand for the proposition for which President Trump cites it. Paul Campos, *That was a right pretty speech, sir. But I ask you, what is a contract?*, Lawyers, Guns & Money (Feb. 8, 2021).

[103] H. Rep. No. 116-346 at 57 (citing 2 J. Story, *Commentaries on the Constitution of the United States*, 268 (1833)).

corruption of the office and of elections.[104] As Alexander Hamilton explained in the *Federalist Papers*, impeachable offenses are defined by "the abuse or violation of some public trust"; they "are of a nature which may with peculiar propriety be denominated POLITICAL, as they relate chiefly to injuries done immediately to the society itself."[105] For these reasons, a "'requirement of criminality would be incompatible with the intent of the [F]ramers to provide a mechanism broad enough to maintain the integrity of constitutional government.'"[106]

History and precedent confirm that conduct need not be criminal to be impeachable. Judge Archbald, for instance, was removed in 1912 for non-criminal speculation in coal properties, and Judge Ritter was removed in 1936 for the non-criminal act of bringing his court into scandal and disrepute.[107] Likewise, the House Judiciary Committee's allegations against President Nixon contained claims encompassing non-criminal acts, although President Nixon resigned before the House itself could consider impeachment.[108] In accord with that precedent, the Senate has also

---

[104] *Id.* (citing Peter Charles Hoffer & N. E. H. Hull, *Impeachment in America, 1635–1805*, at 1-95 (1984), and Frank O. Bowman, III, *High Crimes and Misdemeanors: A History of Impeachment for the Age of Trump*, at 244 (2019)).

[105] Alexander Hamilton, Federalist No. 65; *see also* Joseph Story, *Commentaries on the Constitution of the United States* § 801 (R. Rotunda & J. Nowak eds., 1987) (explaining that impeachment is a political, not a criminal proceeding, intended "not … to punish an offender" by threatening deprivation of his life or liberty, but rather to "secure the state" by "divest[ing] him of his political capacity"); H. Rep. No. 116-346 at 62.

[106] Staff of H. Comm. on the Judiciary, *Constitutional Grounds for Presidential Impeachment 93d Cong.*, at 25 (Comm. Print 1974).

[107] H. Rep. No. 116-346 at 58 (citing *Report of the Committee on the Judiciary, Robert W. Archbald, Judge of the United States Commerce Court*, H. Rep. No. 62–946 (1912), and H. Res. 422, 74th Cong. (1936)).

[108] *Id.* (citing *Committee Report on Nixon Articles of Impeachment* (1974)).

consistently rejected suggestions that it adopt a standard of proof borrowed from the criminal law, choosing instead to allow each Senator to determine how best to judge the facts presented.[109]

While President Trump's efforts to overturn the results of the 2020 election, culminating in his incitement of the January 6 insurrection, very well may have violated the criminal law, that is beside the point here. The only question before the Senate is whether President Trump's violation of his oath and breach of the public trust warrant conviction and disqualification from future officeholding. Here, there is no doubt that it does. Indeed, it is difficult to imagine conduct more deserving of conviction and disqualification than that for which President Trump was impeached.

F. The Article Does Not Charge Multiple Instances Of Impeachable Conduct

President Trump finally errs in arguing that the article of impeachment impermissibly charges "multiple alleged wrongs" and that, as a result, it would be "impossible" for a conviction to comply with the Constitutional requirement that it rest on a two-thirds vote of the Senators present.[110] This argument misconstrues the text of the article and the relevant precedent.

The article does not, as President Trump claims, charge multiple impeachable offenses. Rather, it charges that President Trump engaged in a single course of impeachable conduct in inciting an insurrection on January 6. While the article explains that President Trump employed

---

109 *See, e.g.*, 132 Cong. Rec. S15489-S15490 (daily ed. Oct. 7, 1986) (in his 1986 impeachment proceedings, Judge Harry E. Claiborne moved to designate "beyond a reasonable doubt" as the standard of proof for his conviction; the Senate rejected that request, and one of the House managers explained that the Senate had historically allowed each Member to exercise his or her own personal judgment in impeachment cases); *Report of the Senate Impeachment Trial Committee on the Articles Against Judge Alcee Hastings: Hearings before the Senate Impeachment Trial Committee* (Part 1) 101st Cong., 1st Sess. 73-75 (when a question arose about the appropriate standard of proof during the 1989 impeachment of Judge Alcee Hastings, a Senator explained that there was no set standard; rather "[i]t is what is in the mind of every Senator.... it is what everybody decides for themselves").

110 Opp. at 71-72; *see also* U.S. Const., Art. I § 3, cl. 6 (conviction requires "the Concurrence of two thirds of the Members present"); Rule XXIII, *Rules of Procedure and Practice in the Senate When Sitting on Impeachment Trials* (rev. Aug. 16, 1986) (providing that articles of impeachment may not be "divisible for the purpose of voting thereon").

various tactics, over the course of months, "to subvert and obstruct the certification of the results of the 2020 Presidential election," it also makes clear that these activities merely provided the kindling, which President Trump set aflame when he incited insurrection on January 6.[111] Of course, this prior course of conduct is also relevant in illuminating President Trump's state of mind on January 6 when he exhorted his followers to march to the Capitol and "fight like hell."

President Trump appears to borrow his argument from a similar one made (unsuccessfully) during the impeachment trial of President Clinton.[112] But any comparison to President Clinton's impeachment does not help President Trump here. The articles in President Clinton's impeachment charged that he engaged in "one or more" improper acts.[113] Thus, unlike this article, the Senate could have convicted President Clinton without a two-thirds agreement on which of the charged improper acts he committed. Even so, the Senate *rejected* President Clinton's effort to dismiss the articles on the ground that they charged multiple offenses.[114] As the House Managers explained, the Senate's Rules (which remain in effect today) "specifically contemplate that the House may draft articles of impeachment" containing multiple specifications, "and prior rulings of the Senate have

---

[111] H. Res. 24, 117th Cong. (2021).

[112] Opp. at 71 (quoting the 2020 Trial Memorandum of President Donald J. Trump (at 107-108), which in turn invoked the "duplicity" argument made during the Clinton impeachment trial).

[113] H. Res. 611, 105th Cong. (1998).

[114] 145 Cong. Rec. S961, S973-S974 (daily ed. Jan. 25, 1999).

held that such drafting is not deficient."[115] If President Clinton's claim failed—where the articles in fact alleged multiple, distinct acts of impeachable conduct—then so too must President Trump's.

* * *

[115] *Reply of United States House of Representatives to Trial Memorandum of President William Jefferson Clinton* (Jan. 14, 1999) [145 Cong. Rec. S215-21 (daily ed. Jan. 14, 1999)] at 25 (*reprinted in Proceedings of the United States Senate in the Impeachment Trial of President William Jefferson Clinton*, S. Doc. 106-4, 106th Cong., 1st Sess. (Feb. 12, 1999)); *see also Amending the Rules of Procedure and Practice in the Senate When Sitting on Impeachment Trials*, Report of the Comm. on Rules and Administration, S. Rep. No. 99-401, 99th Cong., 2nd Sess., at 8 (1986) (recognizing that "the most judicious and efficacious" approach to drafting articles of impeachment would be to present "broadly based charges" containing multiple enumerated specifications, and noting that the new rules would allow for conviction where a Senator found the accused guilty "of one or more of the enumerated specifications").

IN THE SENATE OF THE UNITED STATES
Sitting as a Court of Impeachment

In re **IMPEACHMENT OF** **PRESIDENT DONALD J. TRUMP**

REPLY MEMORANDUM OF THE UNITED STATES HOUSE OF REPRESENTATIVES IN THE IMPEACHMENT TRIAL OF PRESIDENT DONALD J. TRUMP

United States House of Representatives

Jamie Raskin
Diana DeGette
David Cicilline
Joaquin Castro
Eric Swalwell
Ted Lieu
Stacey Plaskett
Madeleine Dean
Joe Neguse

U.S. House of Representatives Managers